FOOTPATHS OF BRITAIN

SOUTH-WEST

ENGLAND

Marks and Spencer p.l.c.
Baker Street, London, W1U 8EP
www.marksandspencer.com

Copyright © Exclusive Editions 2004

Created and produced by
The Bridgewater Book Company Ltd
Designer Alison Hughes
Editor Martyn Oliver
Map artwork Richard Constable, John Fowler, Ginny Zeal

ISBN: 1-84461-057-8
Printed in China

www.walkingworld.com

Visit the Walkingworld website at www.walkingworld.com

All the walks in this book are available in more detailed form on the
Walkingworld website. The route instructions have photographs at key
decision points to help you navigate, and each walk comes with an
Ordnance Survey® map. Simply print them out on A4 paper and you are
ready to go! A modest annual subscription gives you access to over 1,400
walks, all in this easy-to-follow format. If you wish, you can purchase
individual walks for a small fee.

Next to every walk in this book you will see a Walk ID. You can enter this
ID number on Walkingworld's 'Find a Walk' page and you will be taken
straight to the details of that walk.

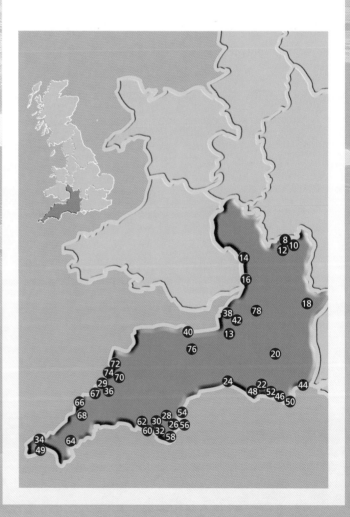

CONTENTS

Introduction

Britain is a fabulous place to walk. We are blessed with a varied and beautiful landscape, a dense network of public footpaths and places of historical interest at every corner. Add to all this the many thousands of well-placed pubs, tea shops and visitor attractions, and it's easy to see why walking is a treasured pastime for millions of people.

Walking is the perfect way to keep fit and healthy. It is good for your heart, muscles and body generally, without making the extreme demands of many sports. For most walkers, however, the health benefits are secondary. We walk for the sheer pleasure of it — being able to breathe in the fresh air, enjoy the company of our friends and 'get away from it all'.

Equipment

If you take up walking as a hobby, it is quite possible to spend a fortune on specialist outdoor kit. But you really don't need to. Just invest in a few inexpensive basics and you'll be ready to enjoy any of the walks in this book.

For footwear, walking boots are definitely best as they provide you with ankle support and protection from the inevitable mud, nettles and puddles. A lightweight pair should be fine if you have no intention of venturing up big hills or over rugged terrain. If you are not sure what to get, go to a specialist shop and ask for advice. Above all, choose boots that fit well and are comfortable.

Take clothing to deal with any weather that you may encounter. Allow for the 'wind-chill' factor – if your clothes get wet you will feel this cooling effect even more. Carry a small rucksack with a spare top, a hat and waterproofs, just in case. The key is being able to put on and take off layers of clothing at will and so keep an even, comfortable temperature throughout the day.

It's a good idea to carry some food and drink. Walking is exercise and you need to replace the fluid you lose through perspiration. Take a bottle of soft drink or water, and sip it regularly rather than downing it in one go. The occasional chocolate bar, sandwich or biscuit can work wonders when energy levels are flagging.

Walking poles – the modern version of the walking stick – are worth considering. They help you to balance and allow your arms to take some of the strain when going uphill. They also lessen the impact on your knees on downhill slopes. Don't be fooled into thinking that poles are just for the older walker – they are popular with trekkers and mountaineers of all ages.

Finding your way

Most walkers use Ordnance Survey® maps, rightly considered to be among the most accurate, up-to-date and 'walker-friendly' in the world. All areas of England, Scotland and Wales are covered by the detailed 1:25,000 scale Explorer and Explorer OL map series. These include features such as field boundaries, farm buildings and small streams.

Having a map and compass – and learning how to use them – is vital to being safe in the countryside. Compass and map skills come with practice – there is no substitute for taking them out and having a go. It is a good idea to purchase a compass with a transparent base plate and rotating dial; you will find this type in any outdoor shop. Most compasses come with simple instructions – if the one you buy does not, ask in the shop for a guide.

If this all sounds a bit too serious for you, I urge you not to worry too much about getting lost. We have all done it – some of us more often than we care to admit! You are unlikely to come to much harm unless you are on a featureless hilltop or out in very poor weather. If you want to build up your confidence, start with shorter routes through farmland or along the coastline and allow yourself plenty of time.

key to maps

☏	Telephone		Lighthouse
ⓘ	Start of walk		Camping
	Viewpoint	▲	Youth hostel
△	Pylon		Bridge
	Triangulation point		Windmill
	Radio mast		Highest point/summit
	Church with Steeple	PH	Public house
	Church without Steeple	PC	Public convenience
	Chapel	1666	Place of historical interest
	Power lines		Embankment
⚑	Golf course		Rocky area/ sharp drop
	Picnic area	■	Building
	Car park		Castle
	Information	☆	Tumulus
			Garden

There are plenty of walks in this book that are perfect for the beginner. You can make navigating even easier by downloading the routes in this book from Walkingworld's website: www.walkingworld.com. These detailed walk instructions feature a photograph at each major decision point, to help you confirm your position and see where to go next.

Another alternative is to join a local walking group

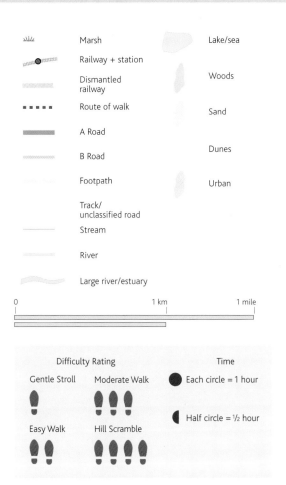

⊥⊥⊥	Marsh			Lake/sea
▣	Railway + station			Woods
	Dismantled railway			
▪ ▪ ▪ ▪	Route of walk			Sand
▬▬▬	A Road			Dunes
	B Road			
	Footpath			Urban
──	Track/ unclassified road			
──	Stream			
⋯⋯	River			
～～	Large river/estuary			

```
0                    1 km              1 mile
```

Difficulty Rating   Time

Gentle Stroll   Moderate Walk   ● Each circle = 1 hour

👣   👣👣👣   ◗ Half circle = ½ hour

Easy Walk   Hill Scramble

👣👣   👣👣👣

and learn from others. There are hundreds of such groups around the country, with members keen to share their experience and skills.

Enough words. Take the walks in this book as your inspiration. Grab your map and compass, and put on your boots. It's time to go out and walk!

Have fun.

DAVID STEWART *Walkingworld*

▲ Map: Explorer 45
▲ Distance: 6 km/3¾ miles
▲ Walk ID: 1663 Wendy Pickler

Difficulty rating

Time

▲ Hills or Fells, National Trust/NTS,
Wildlife, Birds, Flowers, Great Views,
Butterflies, Woodland, Ancient Monument

Dover's Hill from Weston-sub-Edge

This walk begins at Weston-sub-Edge, nestling at the foot of the Cotswold escarpment, then climbs Dover's Hill with its breathtaking views, before returning to the village with a pleasant stroll down through the woods.

1 From Parson's Lane take the field footpath between the gardens. Follow it as it bends right and then turn left in front of the driveway onto a grass path. Turn left over the wooden footbridge and go through the kissing gate.

2 At the telegraph pole, pass to the right and head up to the field's top right-hand corner, where you cross two stiles in quick succession. Turn right and immediately left through a metal gate. Follow the field's left boundary, crossing over a stile in the hedge ahead. Continue in the same direction, then turn left to cross the stile and footbridge. Follow the right hedge and ditch to a metal gate, but turn left away from this and head up the hill to the right of two large oak trees. Cross the driveway, following the signpost up the hill.

3 Aim for the stile in the field's top right-hand corner, cross over and continue walking in the same direction, with the fence on your left. Cross two adjoining stiles and continue uphill, bearing slightly right to pass through a kissing gate. Follow the signs to the road, then turn right up the hill.

4 When you reach the kissing gate on the left, cross over into the National Trust property of Dover's Hill and head right up the slope to the top (about 230 m). From here, walk along the escarpment, which falls away on the

The view from Dover's Hill is superb. Here we see Meon Hill in the distance.

left, and continue downhill past the trig point, until the path eventually arrives at a field gate.

5 Rather than go through the gate, turn left and continue to proceed downhill towards the woodland, keeping close to the right-hand hedge. Ignore the kissing gate to the left and cross over the stile in the corner, following the path signposted to Weston into the woodland. Walk ahead, keeping to the lower (right) path and following the yellow waymarks to cross a stile into a field. Head downhill with the fence on your left, turn left at the fence corner, and continue towards the end of the field.

further information

Dover's Hill takes its name from Robert Dover who in 1612 held the first 'Cotswold Olimpicks'. The tradition is maintained today with a festival of sport and pageantry held annually on the Friday evening after the spring bank holiday.

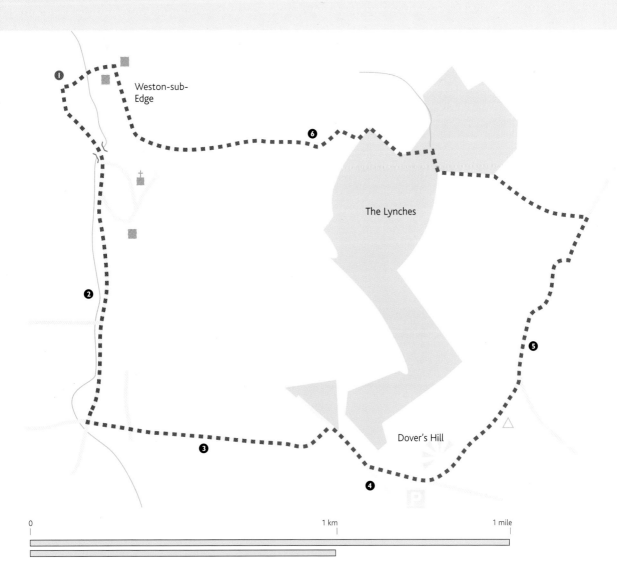

Weston-sub-Edge

The Lynches

Dover's Hill

0   1 km   1 mile

❻ Before you reach the field's end, turn half-right to cross the stile and walk between the trees to a second stile. Cross this and walk between the fences. You eventually pass through a kissing gate. Walk diagonally across the field, keeping to the left of the nearest goalpost. Cross over the stile and head to a stile and gate in the far right-hand corner by the road. Turn right along the road and then left into Parson's Lane and back to the start.

access information

From Stratford, take the B4632 towards Broadway. At Weston-sub-Edge, turn left up the road signed Dover's Hill. Look out for Parson's Lane on the right. The walk begins near the end of Parson's Lane on the left. There is limited parking along this road.

▲ Map: Explorer 45

▲ Distance: 6 km/3¾ miles

▲ Walk ID: 1628 Ron and Jenny Glynn

Difficulty rating

Time

▲ Hills or Fells, Pub, Toilets, Church, Stately Home, National Trust/NTS, Wildlife, Birds, Flowers, Great Views, Butterflies, Food Shop, Tea Shop, Woodland

Snowshill Circular

This charming little circuit around Snowshill village and Manor takes in glorious views over the valley and of rich farmland stretching away in the far distance. Snowshill Manor is owned by The National Trust.

❶ From the car park in the village, turn left onto the road towards the manor. Cross the stile at the manor entrance and walk downhill towards the trees. Pass through the kissing gate and then bear left over the uneven terrain to reach the gate.

❷ Go through the gate and walk down the slope to a second gate below, bearing left. Once through this gate, cross the footbridge over the stream to join the woodland path. Follow the path round the edge of the field, climbing steadily, then cross the stile into pastureland and follow the fence on the left-hand side. Snowshill Manor sits on the valley slope over to the left. Continue to walk along the tree-lined ridge.

❸ At the kissing gate, turn right onto the bridle track that runs alongside the wood, overlooking the valley on the right. Walk on until you come to a large metal gate on your left.

❹ Cross the stile by the gate, then turn right up the slope. Continue down to the fence. Ignoring the stile on the right, walk on through the metal gate, then uphill between the fences, passing two junctions and disused quarries. Further on, you pass a right turning and gate leading to another path. Ignore these and continue along the edge of the wood.

❺ Turn left into Littleworth Wood, a National Trust area, and keep to the main path. At the fork, turn right and cross the stile to leave the wood. Bear left down to the gate below, with the buildings of Snowshill on the hillside before you. Turn right onto the hard track.

❻ When you come to a junction, turn left and walk past two large houses to the road. Turn left at the road down to Snowshill village. The road takes you past St Barnabas church and Snowshill Manor to complete the circuit.

Snowshill Manor, a fine house built of Cotswold stone, with a delightful organic garden.

further information

Snowshill Manor houses the unique collection, amassed during the first half of the 20th century, of the eccentric, Charles Paget Wade.

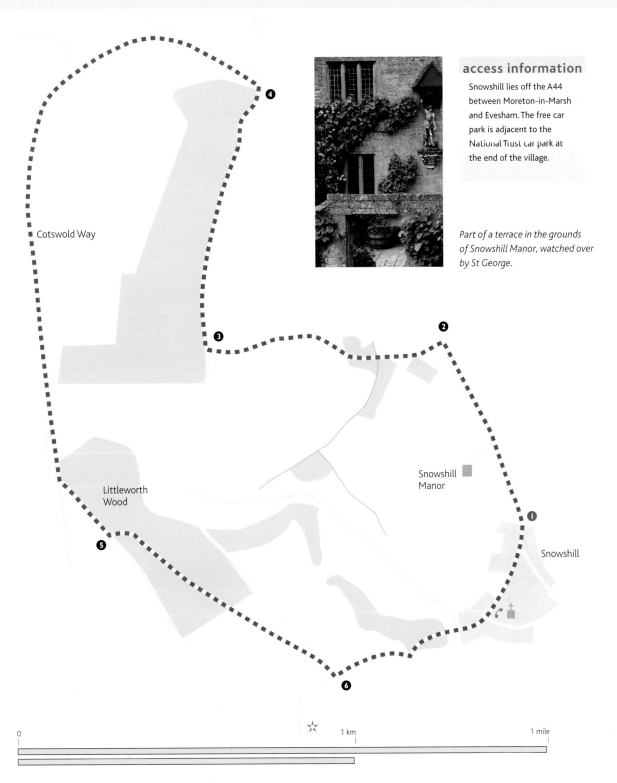

Cotswold Way

4

3

2

Snowshill
Manor

1

Littleworth
Wood

Snowshill

5

6

access information

Snowshill lies off the A44 between Moreton-in-Marsh and Evesham. The free car park is adjacent to the National Trust car park at the end of the village.

Part of a terrace in the grounds of Snowshill Manor, watched over by St George.

0   1 km   1 mile

▲ Map: Explorer 141
▲ Distance: 5 km/3 miles
▲ Walk ID: 1081 Tony Brotherton

Difficulty rating

Time

▲ Hills or Fells, Pub, Toilets, Museum, National Trust, Wildlife, Birds, Flowers, Great Views, Butterflies, Food Shop, Tea Shop

Around Glastonbury

A short tour of the town, including optional visits to the Abbey Ruins and Glastonbury Thorn, the Chalice Well and other points of religious interest, plus the obligatory pilgrimage to the Tor.

❶ From the car park in Magdalene Street turn right, passing the entrance to the Abbey. Turn right onto the High Street. Walk up the High Street, passing the tourist information office on the left (the Lake Village Museum is housed here). Continue past St John's Church. Turn right along Lambrook Street, and carry on as far as the gateway of Abbey House on the right.

❷ Turn up Dod Lane and take the driveway on the right, signed 'Footpath to Tor', to reach a squeeze stile. Follow the path uphill through fields to a lane and continue ahead.

❸ Turn left to follow Bulwarks Lane to its end. At the road (Wick Hollow), turn uphill to reach the crossroads.

❹ Take the lane to the right, with the Tor visible ahead, to reach a junction. Turn left and continue as far as the footpath to the Tor. Follow the path into a field, soon to climb to a stepped path. The path rises steeply to reach the summit and monument, where there are superb views.

❺ Descend the Tor to reach a metal gate. Take the footpath downhill to Well House Lane. Turn left, then right at the road to arrive at Chalice Well. Turn right along Chilkwell Street to reach, on the left at the junction with Bere Lane, the Somerset Rural Life Museum.

❻ Turn left onto Bere Lane, then right downhill at the crossroads to return to Magdalene Street, to visit Alsmhouses Chapel. Turn left and continue past the former pumphouse to return to the start of the walk.

further information

Glastonbury was the first Christian sanctuary in Britain and is the legendary burial-place of King Arthur. The abbey ruins are open every day (except Christmas Day) from 9.30 a.m. to 6 p.m. (or dusk if earlier).

Chalice Well is open every day – visiting times vary according to the season, so check beforehand if you wish to visit. The waters of the well were once considered curative.

The Somerset Rural Life Museum is open 10 a.m. to 5 p.m., Tuesday to Friday, April to October, and at weekends from 2 to 6 p.m.

The Mump, the distinctive and extraordinary mound of Glastonbury Tor, can be spotted from miles away.

access information

Glastonbury is on the A361. Park in Magdalene Street, adjacent to Glastonbury Abbey grounds.

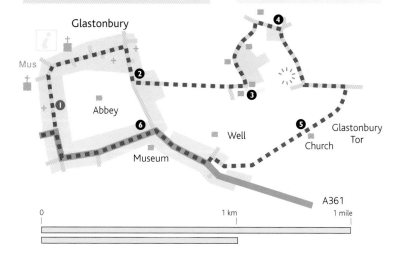

Glastonbury

Mus

Abbey

Museum

Well

Church

Glastonbury Tor

A361

0   1 km   1 mile

▲ Map: Explorer OL 45
▲ Distance: 5 km/3 miles
▲ Walk ID: 108 John Stewart

Difficulty rating

Time

▲ Hills or Fells, Great Views, Wildlife, Birds, Flowers

Beckbury Monument from Stanway

This circular walk in the heart of the Cotswolds involves a gentle climb up the escarpment to a point with a superb view. The return follows a section of The Cotswold Way.

1 From the Stanway crossroads, take the minor road heading right to Wood Stanway. Continue on this road and take the left fork. Turn right onto the lane at the start of Wood Stanway, then turn right beyond the cottage on the right.

2 Go through the gate and turn sharp left. Head over the meadow towards the wood. Follow the grassy track uphill, keeping the wood on the right. Where the wood ends, cross the stile and turn sharp left, continuing towards the top of a steep bank.

3 On top of the bank is a monument and viewpoint. Just to the back of the monument go through the wooden gate towards Beckbury Camp and continue on the grassy track, with the edge of the escarpment on the left. The path soon turns sharp right following the field boundary, terminating at a stony lane. Turn left and follow the track.

4 At the road, turn left through the wooden gate onto a grassy path. The path descends the escarpment towards Wood Stanway. After a metal gate turn

right and continue downhill, keeping the wall on your right. Follow the yellow markers over several stiles. Continue as the path meanders towards the village. At the valley bottom go through the metal gate onto the stony track. Pass the farm buildings and cottages.

5 After the cottages turn right at the metal gate. Follow the path, keeping the field boundaries on the left until reaching a road. Turn left and continue to the start of walk.

Sheep graze in verdant, rolling countryside, in the Cotswolds near Stow-on-the-Wold.

access information

The walk starts at the Stanway crossroads on the B4077 road north-west from Stow-on-the-Wold. There is good but limited off-road parking just south of the crossroads on the minor road leading to Wood Stanway.

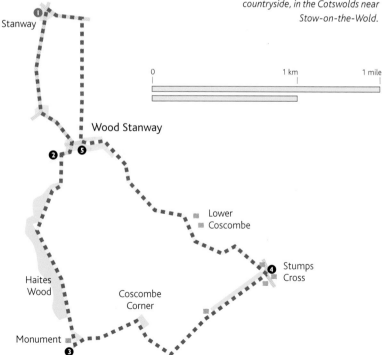

▲ Map: Explorer 14
▲ Distance: 6 km/3¾ miles
▲ Walk ID: 1606 Pat Roberts

Difficulty rating

Time

▲ Hills or Fells, National Trust/NTS, Wildlife, Birds, Flowers, Great Views, Butterflies, Woodland, Ancient Monument

The Kymin and Wysis Way

The highlight of this relaxed walk on the border between England and Wales is the view from The Kymin: on a clear day you can see right across to the Welsh Mountains, over Monmouth and the Wye and Usk Valleys.

❶ Walk down to the road from the lay-by, and head west towards Monmouth on the wide grass verge. At Duke of York Road, turn left. This is a very quiet, 'no-through' lane.

❷ Where the road swings sharp left, look for a lane going up between the hedges. There is a telegraph pole on the left and a signpost on the right marking the entrance. Turn into this lane and stay with it as it bends and drops down to a T-junction with a gravel track, then continue left and up.

❸ You come to a stile on the left just before the track flattens out. The stile itself is marked 'Wysis' and there is a signpost to The Kymin near by. Go through the stile and follow the grass path up the field to a stile and gate. The route then bears left, up to open ground. Head for slightly left of the masts, visible in the trees on the skyline.

The Wysis Way winds through the Forest of Dean, below, eventually reaching the source of the Thames 90 km away.

4 Cross the stile into the grounds of The Kymin. There is a National Trust sign behind the stile. For a rest and to enjoy the view, make for the bench at the Roundhouse. There is also an information board here. As you face the mountains, the Naval Temple is on your left. To resume the walk, return to the stile and walk back down over the open ground, cross the stile and gate and return to waymark 3. Proceed down the gravel path until you reach the A4136.

5 At the road, cross over and look for the sign for Wysis Way slightly to the left. Follow this narrow path down through the trees to a wide gravel path,

access information

Park in the large lay-by on the A4136 Monmouth to Staunton road, opposite an information board on the Forest of Dean. There is a good bus service from Monmouth or Cinderford.

further information

The Naval Temple at The Kymin was built in 1800 by the people of Monmouth to celebrate the victories of the British Navy and Admirals. It was visited in 1802 by Nelson, who commented favourably on the view.

where it veers right and slightly down. Ignore the track coming up from the left, and gradually swing right and up until you come to a T-junction with a forest track. Turn right and head back to the A4136. At the road, turn right again towards the lay-by.

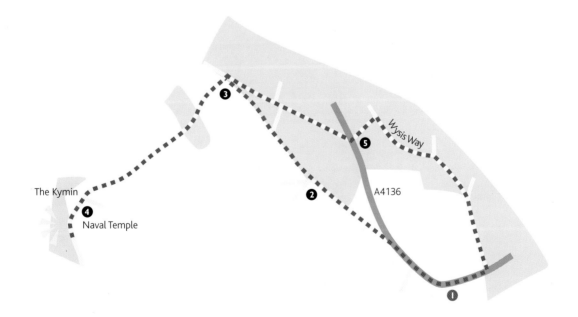

The Kymin

4 Naval Temple

3

5

Wysis Way

2

A4136

1

0   1 km   1 mile

▲ Map: Explorer OL 14
▲ Distance: 5 km/3 miles
▲ Walk ID: 1426 Pat Roberts

Difficulty rating

Time

▲ Wildlife, Birds, Flowers, Great Views,
Butterflies, Mostly Flat, Woodland

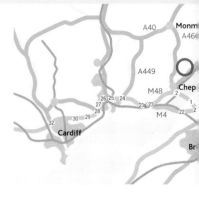

Poors Allotment and the Jubilee Stone from Tidenham Chase

This easy, fairly level walk rewards you with fine views over the Severn Estuary to the Cotswolds to visit the Jubilee Stone.

1 Leave the car park and turn left onto the road. After 120 m, at the footpath sign, go right and continue through a series of gates to reach a minor road. Turn right.

2 Where the road swings sharply right, take the gate next to the footpath signs and follow the sign on the left. Head diagonally left, towards a stile in a fence. Cross the stile onto Poors Allotment, taking in the views over the Severn Estuary to the left.

3 Cross a small stream. Just before the large holly tree, the main path swings to the right. Ignore this path and head left, then turn left into the wood. Emerge from the wood into open ground and swing sharp right to reach a yellow marker post and then cross a stile onto a road. Turn left. After about 150 m, head right, past a barrier and into heathland, small trees and gorse. As the Gloucester Way comes in from the left, continue with it on the path furthest on the left.

4 At the Jubilee Stone, turn right and continue, ignoring any minor paths until you reach a clearing. At the clearing, ignore the track that comes in from the left and take the narrow path that goes off to the right. Follow this path through the wood. Ignore paths off to the left and the main road. When you reach a minor road, turn left.

5 Just before the main road take the stone stile on the right onto Poors Allotment. Stay on this grass track as it moves away from the trees and road on your left.

6 At the junction of paths, take the left fork, heading towards the trees and into the wood. Emerge from the wood through a metal kissing gate at the roadside opposite the car park.

access information

Parking is in an area adjoining the B4228, north-east of Chepstow. There is a roadside sign to Offa's Dyke.

A view of the Severn Bridge, built across the Severn Estuary to provide a link between Wales and England, can be enjoyed during this walk.

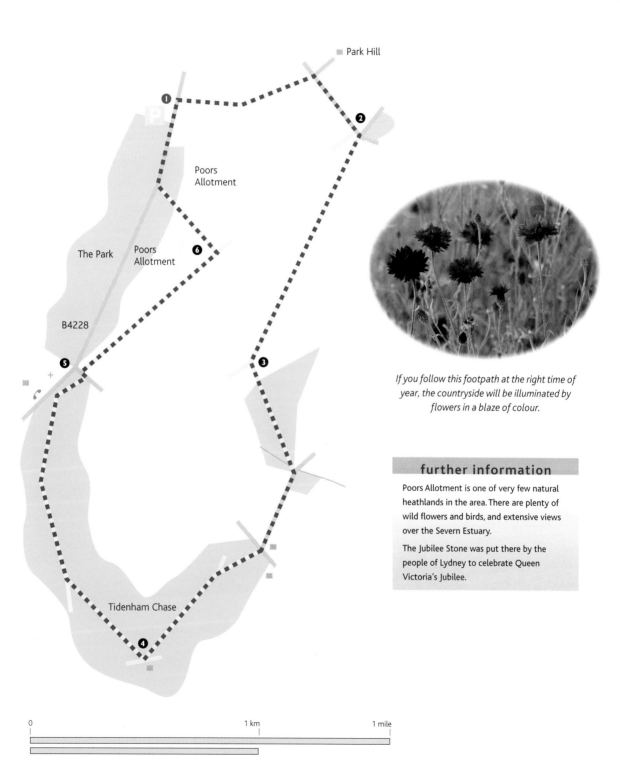

Park Hill

① P

Poors
Allotment

②

The Park Poors
Allotment

⑥

B4228

⑤

③

If you follow this footpath at the right time of
year, the countryside will be illuminated by
flowers in a blaze of colour.

further information

Poors Allotment is one of very few natural
heathlands in the area. There are plenty of
wild flowers and birds, and extensive views
over the Severn Estuary.

The Jubilee Stone was put there by the
people of Lydney to celebrate Queen
Victoria's Jubilee.

Tidenham Chase

④

| 0 | 1 km | 1 mile |

▲ Map: Explorer 157
▲ Distance: 8.5 km/5¼ miles
▲ Walk ID: 68 David Stewart

Difficulty rating

Time

▲ Pub, Museum, National Trust/NTS, Gift Shop, Restaurant, Great Views

The Sanctuary, West Kennet Long Barrow and Silbury Hill from Avebury

From the Avebury stone circle, this walk goes along the Stone Avenue and up to the Ridgeway with its views of 'hedgehogs' and curious burial mounds. The route then visits The Sanctuary, the West Kennet Long Barrow and Silbury Hill burial ground.

❶ From the car park, follow the signs to Avebury village. At the road, turn right into the ring. Follow the ring round to the left. Cross the main road into the next part of the ring. Bear right and climb up onto the bank. Go down the other side towards a gate. Cross the road into the field. Walk down Stone Avenue between the stones.

❷ At the end of Stone Avenue go through a gate, cross the road, and follow the path opposite. Keeping on the same side of the hedge, cross into the next field. Follow the left-hand field edge slightly uphill to the next field boundary.

❸ Turn right on the track leading towards the 'hedgehogs', a clump of trees on the horizon. Follow the path as it bears left after the hedgehogs, then turn right and follow the Ridgeway down to cross the main road.

❹ Visit The Sanctuary on the right, then follow the path signed 'Byway', directly opposite the end of the Ridgeway. Just before the path turns left and crosses a bridge, turn right and follow the path alongside the river to a road.

access information

Avebury lies halfway between Marlborough and Calne, just off the A4. The National Trust provides a free car park just before reaching Avebury village on the A4361. Buses are available from Devizes, Marlborough and Swindon (Wiltshire Bus Line, 0345 090899).

A fine aerial view of Avebury village. Strong shadows throw the ancient stone circle into relief.

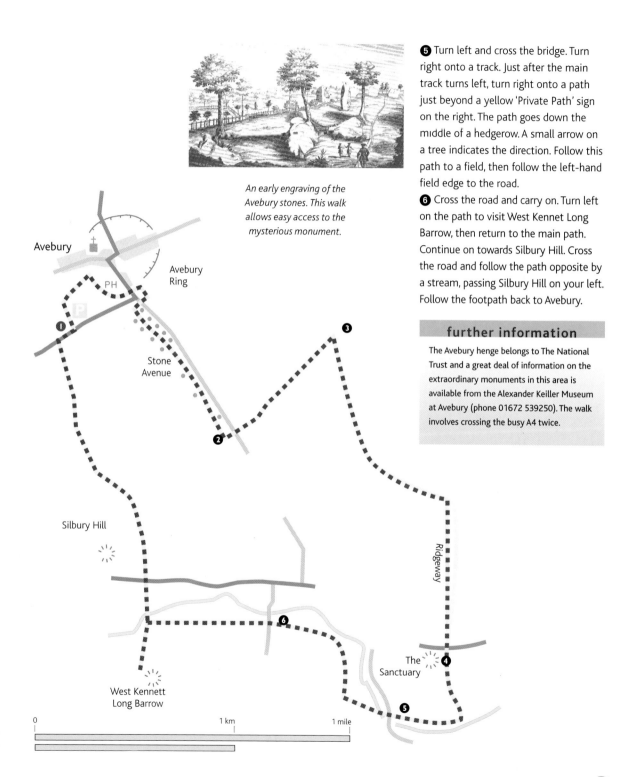

An early engraving of the Avebury stones. This walk allows easy access to the mysterious monument.

5 Turn left and cross the bridge. Turn right onto a track. Just after the main track turns left, turn right onto a path just beyond a yellow 'Private Path' sign on the right. The path goes down the middle of a hedgerow. A small arrow on a tree indicates the direction. Follow this path to a field, then follow the left-hand field edge to the road.

6 Cross the road and carry on. Turn left on the path to visit West Kennet Long Barrow, then return to the main path. Continue on towards Silbury Hill. Cross the road and follow the path opposite by a stream, passing Silbury Hill on your left. Follow the footpath back to Avebury.

further information

The Avebury henge belongs to The National Trust and a great deal of information on the extraordinary monuments in this area is available from the Alexander Keiller Museum at Avebury (phone 01672 539250). The walk involves crossing the busy A4 twice.

Avebury

Avebury Ring

Stone Avenue

Silbury Hill

Ridgeway

The Sanctuary

West Kennett Long Barrow

0   1 km   1 mile

▲ Map: Explorer 118
▲ Distance: 10.7 km/6¾ miles
▲ Walk ID: 486 Al Rodger

Difficulty rating

Time
● ● ●

▲ Hills, Pub, Church, Birds, Great Views

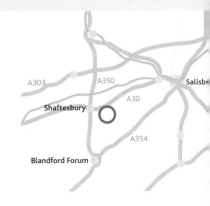

Win Green and Tollard Royal

This peaceful circular walk starts at Win Green Hill, the highest point on Cranborne Chase, with exceptional views. The route follows a tree-lined dry valley to Tollard Royal, then returns on a mostly gradual climb to the main ridgeway.

❶ From the car park, walk towards the clump of trees, passing either side of them to reach the ridgeway. Around the first corner, climb a stile over the right-hand fence into the trees and descend the steep hillside on the path slanting right. The path becomes somewhat indistinct, but aim to keep up from the valley bottom until turning right as the side valley comes in from the right.

❷ Follow the main track over the rise and down the valley, following the marker posts. (The path passes through a cottage garden but to avoid upsetting the occupants, bypass the cottage on the track.) Where the main track bends right, turn left down to the fence, crossing two stiles and going up through a gate to the track along the left side of the valley.

❸ When you meet another track, either walk down into Tollard Royal or head up the track, then turn right and cross a stile to follow a footpath pointer. The path slants left up the hill then crosses fields over the top of the hill.

further information

Cranborne Chase was originally a royal hunting ground, popular with King John, and run by the Lord of the Chase. Privately owned from the 1600s to 1830, the Lord of the Chase owned the deer and game which, along with the woods they bred in, were protected. Tolls were charged during fawning and crop damage caused by hunters went uncompensated.

❹ Cross a stile beside a gate and follow the path slanting down the hill to the left to join a track in the valley bottom. Go through a gate and climb up the track ahead. At the next fence line, follow the track round to the right and through a gate alongside trees, keeping out of the field.

❺ Emerging from the wood, follow the route left off the track, then right into the field, heading for the gap in the trees on the skyline. At the crossroads on the top of the ridge, turn left. When the road begins to drop off the ridge, fork left on the track.

❻ At the junction of tracks and road, walk straight on and take the track rising over the hill ahead, meeting the outward route and following the track back to the car park.

access information

From the A30 Shaftesbury to Salisbury road, turn right in Ludwell at the signpost to the Larmer Tree Garden. As you climb onto the Chase, look for a signpost Byway to Win Green on the left, and follow the pot-holed road to the car park.

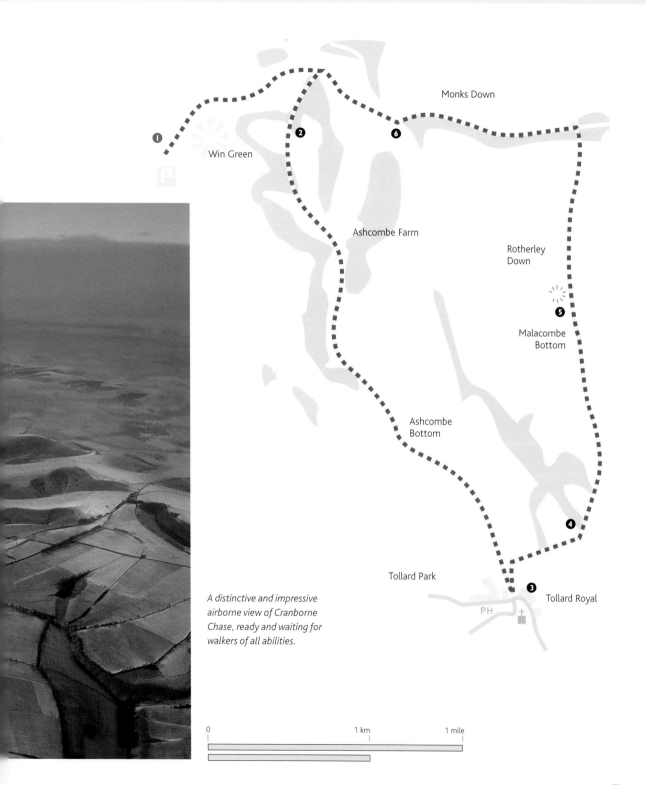

Monks Down

① Win Green

P

②

⑥

Ashcombe Farm

Rotherley Down

⑤

Malacombe Bottom

Ashcombe Bottom

④

A distinctive and impressive airborne view of Cranborne Chase, ready and waiting for walkers of all abilities.

Tollard Park

③ Tollard Royal

PH †

0   1 km   1 mile

▲ Map: Explorer OL 15
▲ Distance: 10 km/6¼ miles
▲ Walk ID: 572 Alan Kingsland

Difficulty rating

Time

▲ Hills or Fells, River, Pub, Church, National Trust, Wildlife, Birds, Flowers, Great Views

Hardy's Chess Piece Monument from Martinstown

This walk starts and finishes at St Martin's Church in the village of Martinstown, Dorset. The walk takes you through some fields and a copse to Great Hill. The walk then follows the ridge to the 'Chess Piece' that is Hardy's Monument.

❶ Cross the road from the church, then the footbridge to continue on a road. Once past the buildings the road bends first left then right. On the right bend join a footpath to the left. From the footpath sign the path leads across the field ahead. On the far side of this field go through a second to reach a young copse. Follow the path to the bottom of the valley. Then keep right as you travel up the valley to a farm track. Turn left, following the track to a field at the bottom of Great Hill.

❷ Take the chalky track up the first slope of Great Hill and into a field. Cross the middle of the field and go through the gate at the end. Continue across the next field to a hedge and signpost. Down to your left are views of Weymouth and Portland. Turn right and follow the path along the field edge and under the power lines. Take the path ahead at the rusty tanks. Go through a gate, up the hill between the gorse bushes to a second gate. Turn right and go through the gate, following the ridge path to the Chess Piece. At the road turn left and follow it up to the car park and monument.

❸ Retrace your steps back to the inland coastal path. Keep on the path to the junction.

❹ Turn left and follow the path to the farm buildings and road. At the road go through the gate and turn left. Follow this road to Pen Barn Farm.

❺ At the farm follow the path to the right, passing in front of the dark barn. Climb to the hilltop. Go through the gate and follow the field-edge path down the slope to the next gate and track.

❻ Turn left onto the track, leaving to the right after a very short distance. Follow the footpath back down the valley to the copse you passed earlier. Retrace your steps to St Martin's Church.

access information

From the A35 roundabout west of Dorchester, follow signposts to Martinstown. Turn right into the village and head for St Martin's Church (500 m on the right).

Located on the highest point of the Blackdown area, the 21-m Hardy's Monument is a landmark for any walker. Its site provides excellent views of the Dorset coast.

This footpath will lead you through some classic Dorset countryside, taking in picturesque villages and farms.

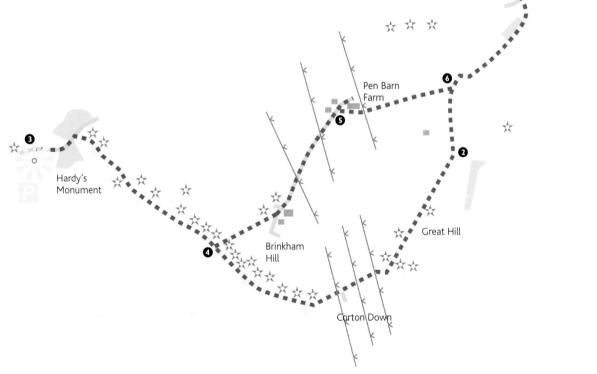

Martinstown

Pen Barn Farm

Hardy's Monument

Brinkham Hill

Great Hill

Corton Down

0   1 km   1 mile

further information

Hardy's Monument was built in 1848 to celebrate the life of Dorset's most famous maritime hero, Sir Thomas Masterman Hardy (of 'Kiss me, Hardy' fame). The monument is owned by The National Trust and is staffed from April to September. The climb to the parapet costs £1.

▲ Map: Explorer 116
▲ Distance: 10 km/6¼ miles
▲ Walk ID: 997 Al Rodger

Difficulty rating

Time

▲ Pub, Church, Wildlife, Birds, Great Views, Butterflies, Woodland

Symondsbury from North Chideock

A303 Yeovil
A3066
Axminster
Lyme Regis Bridport Dor
A35

This is a circular walk through countryside west of Bridport, starting from the village of Chideock, home of the Chideock Martyrs. The route illustrates the charm of West Dorset at its best, and there are wonderful views to enjoy.

❶ Take the track with a cul-de-sac sign beside the cottage. Proceed uphill in a field with a fence on the left. Descend straight down the second field.

❷ Turn right up the hedged track. At the top of the hill continue down the Symondsbury track. Take the road to the left at the school.

❸ Beyond Symondsbury, turn right onto a track. Cross into a field on the left and make for the far-left corner. Cross the bridge and turn right, following the edge of the field to a gate. Cross the track into the field opposite. Cross the field half-left up to the corner of the hedge. Continue with the hedge on your right. At the hole through the hedge, take the path through the trees. Turn right at the junction. On the brow of the hill, turn left for rewarding views.

❹ Continue clockwise round the edge of the hilltop. Take the left path at the first junction. Continue down the steps towards the road and turn left. Turn right up the path between the housing and the hospital. Cross to the right-hand field. Keep ahead to cross back to the left-hand field at the gateway. Continue with the hedge on your right-hand side for two fields.

further information

John Cornelius, the Catholic chaplain of Lady Arundell, was arrested when visiting Chideock in 1594, along with two servants from Chideock and another visitor. The four were found guilty of treason. Refusing to embrace Protestantism, they were executed three months after their arrest.

A cross on the site of Chideock Castle commemorates these martyrs, and two others, Thomas Pilchard and Hugh Green.

The chiselled headlands around Lyme Regis create quite a distinctive coastline that is a fascinating place to explore.

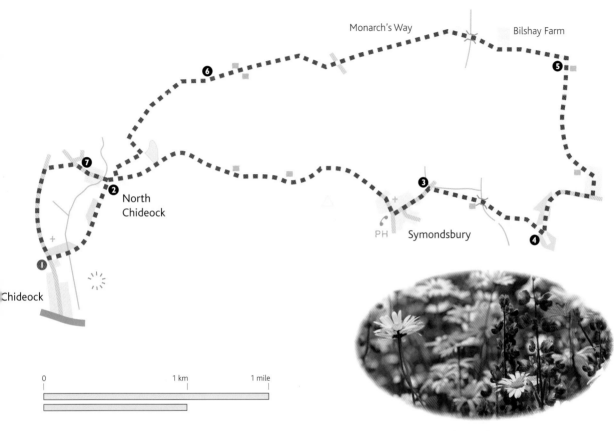

Monarch's Way   Bilshay Farm

6

5

7

2

North
Chideock

3

PH   Symondsbury

4

1

Chideock

0   1 km   1 mile

*Remember to take time to stop
on your walk and 'smell the
flowers'.*

5 At the cottage turn left and follow the hedge. Cross the field to the right-hand of two gates into the next field. Head left towards the electricity pylon. Go over the stile into a garden, following the fence. Descend the field to a gate at the end of a line of posts. Cross the bridge and keep to the right side of the field. Go through the gap in the hedge into the next field. Follow the track up the left side to continue on the Monarch's Way.

6 Go through both gates. Continue down the field and round the thicket on the sheep path. Follow the path and continue down the field towards the hedge, keeping the hedge on the right. Cross the bottom field to the left to reach a stile by a gate. Turn right to follow a track becoming a tarmac lane.

7 Just before the junction, turn up the path on the left. Cross the field to a stile leading down to a path. Turn left at the road and continue back to the start.

▲ Map: Explorer 110
▲ Distance: 8 km/5 miles
▲ Walk ID: 1782 Dennis Blackford

Difficulty rating

Time

River, Pub, Toilets, Museum, Church, Castle, Birds, Flowers, Great Views, Butterflies, Café, Gift Shop, Food Shop, Industrial Archaeology

Totnes from Dartington

This interesting walk passes through the gardens of Dartington Hall and down its long main drive, overlooking the River Dart. The route includes an optional detour along the riverbank to the historic town of Totnes with its castle and museum.

❶ Exit left from the main car parks of the Cider Press Craft Centre at the far end. Cross the road and walk up the lane past the overflow car parks. Follow the tarmac footpath on the right-hand side, round to meet the access road to Dartington Hall.

❷ Where the footpath ends, go through the large white gate into the gardens of Dartington Hall. Follow the wide drive down through the gardens, or take a wander through any of the woodland paths to the right. Near the end of the drive, turn right onto the paved path with the swan fountain. Turn left at the end of this path along the hedged pavement, then right through the hedge and along the terrace in front of the buildings.

❸ At the end of the terrace, go up the first flight of steps, then turn right down another flight to the grass. Note: to look around the buildings, continue up the steps and turn left at the top. Walk for 100 m past the restaurant into the quadrangle. Go out through the arched gateway and turn left onto the road, then left again along the wide path to pass the tranquil Zen Meditation Garden. Go on through the churchyard to rejoin the terrace.

❹ Turn left at the bottom of the steps, and walk along the lawn to its end. Pass through the gate at the bottom of the field and turn right onto the tree-lined main drive. Follow the drive all the way down to the gatehouse.

❺ Pass the gatehouse and go through the gates to turn left onto the river walk. Proceed along this path towards Totnes. Just past the weir, cross the wooden bridge to follow the bank of the river. If you prefer to miss out the river walk, turn right onto the cycle path before you get to the gatehouse, which takes you along the water meadow back to the Craft Centre.

further information

There are toilet facilities and opportunities for refreshment at the Cider Press, Dartington Hall and Totnes.

This is a pushchair-friendly route, with wide tracks and country roads.

A thatched cottage in the beautiful gardens of Dartington Hall.

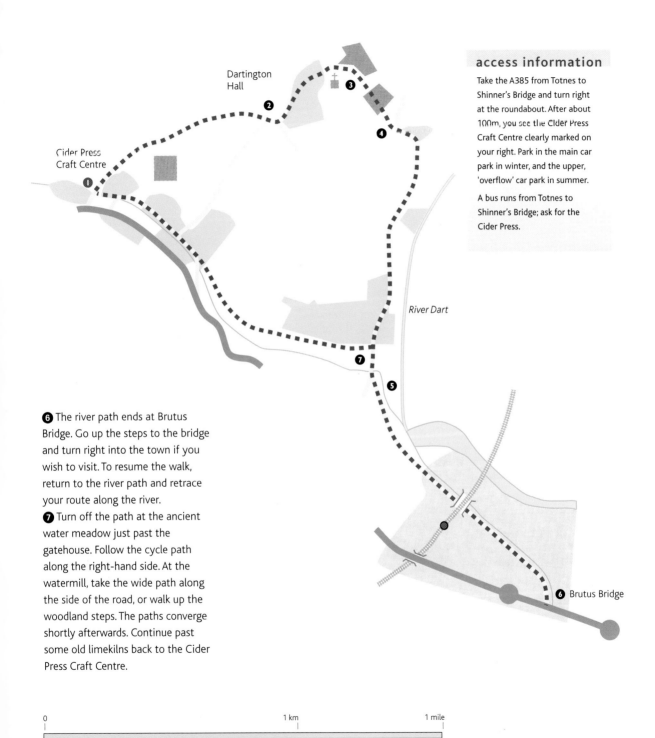

Dartington Hall

Cider Press
Craft Centre

River Dart

access information

Take the A385 from Totnes to Shinner's Bridge and turn right at the roundabout. After about 100m, you see the Cider Press Craft Centre clearly marked on your right. Park in the main car park in winter, and the upper, 'overflow' car park in summer.

A bus runs from Totnes to Shinner's Bridge; ask for the Cider Press.

❻ The river path ends at Brutus Bridge. Go up the steps to the bridge and turn right into the town if you wish to visit. To resume the walk, return to the river path and retrace your route along the river.

❼ Turn off the path at the ancient water meadow just past the gatehouse. Follow the cycle path along the right-hand side. At the watermill, take the wide path along the side of the road, or walk up the woodland steps. The paths converge shortly afterwards. Continue past some old limekilns back to the Cider Press Craft Centre.

❻ Brutus Bridge

0   1 km   1 mile

Difficulty rating

Time

▲ River, Pub, Toilets, Castle, Stately Home, National Trust, Wildlife, Birds, Flowers, Great Views, Butterflies, Woodland

Fingle Bridge from Chagford

This walk is mostly through woodland along the beautiful Teign Valley, with flowers, views and wildlife, and offers the chance to visit Castle Drogo, an early 20th-century Lutyens country house.

1 From the car park walk up the slight rise, passing a stone cottage on your left. Then turn right to go across the farmyard, bearing slightly left to reach a field. The way across the field is marked by a post. Pass through a gate to cross a second field. Go through the next gate into some woodland. Bear right at a sign marked 'Road at Dogmarsh Bridge'. Cross the A382 and enter the Castle Drogo estate by the kissing gate. Walk through the field with the river on your right.

2 Just after entering the woodlands, cross a stile and turn left following the sign 'Hunter's Path'. Walk uphill to pass a thatched cottage on your left, continue ahead on a wider track and then onto a road. When you emerge from the trees with open hillside ahead, turn sharp right through a gate signed 'Castle Drogo and Fingle Bridge'. Follow this path uphill and round a sharp left-hand bend to continue on a path high above the Teign Valley with great views.

3 After a section of open hillside there is a small wooded cleft. Follow the path up some steps. At the road turn left and then bear right to reach the Castle Drogo visitor centre. Retrace your steps back to the path. Continue on the Hunter's Path towards Fingle Bridge. The path descends through oak woods. When you reach the road turn sharp right.

4 Cross the road from The Fingle Bridge Inn and follow the path upstream with the river on your left. After about 1 km you reach point 2. Retrace your steps to the start.

Castle Drogo, designed by Lutyens, is a fake castle built of granite.

access information

Chagford is on the B3206 off the A382 from Newton Abbot. This walk starts at the swimming pool. If no parking is available here, there are several wide areas along the lane to Sandy Park, or there is parking in the village.

further information

Castle Drogo is not a real castle. It is a country house designed by Lutyens in around 1910 for the Drewe family (whose wealth came from the Home & Colonial Stores). It is now owned by The National Trust.

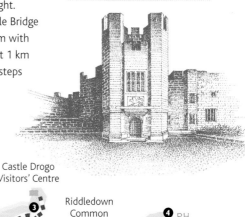

▲ Map: Explorer 111
▲ Distance: 3 km/1¾ miles
▲ Walk ID: 1479 Dennis Blackford

Difficulty rating

Time

▲ River, Church, Wildlife, Birds, Flowers, Great Views, Butterflies, Public Transport, Nature Trail, Waterfall, Woodland, Ancient Monument

The 6th-century chapel of St Piran.

St Nectan's Glen

This circular walk begins from the 6th-century chapel of St Piran and the ancient well, ascending a bridleway to a viewpoint overlooking Tintagel Bay, before descending down into the beautiful wooded valley of St Nectan's Glen.

❶ Start the walk on the public bridleway to the left of the church. Follow this track to the top of the hill.

❷ Go through several gates and follow the track as it turns to the right. As the track descends, look over the hedge to your right for spectacular views of the Tintagel coast. The track ends and a path continues down to the right between the metal gate and the wooden buildings.

❸ At the Hermitage Tea Gardens there is access to a waterfall. After visiting the waterfall, take the path to the right of the gardens, which leads down into St Nectan's Glen. Ignore all other paths and descend the steps. The path levels out and runs along the gorge. The path descends down more steps to reach the valley floor. Continue along the path beside the river. Follow the path across the river by a wooden bridge before crossing back via a concrete one. Where the path branches, ignore the path over the bridge and keep to the right-hand side of the river.

❹ After ascending again, the path emerges onto an access road. Follow the road back to the church.

further information

St Piran's Well is opposite the small car park near the start of the walk. The well would have dated back many hundreds of years before St Piran's name was attached to it.

access information

Take the B3263 from Tintagel or Boscastle to the Rocky Valley Inn approximately midway between the two, where you will find a concrete bus shelter on the seaward side of the road and a car park near by. By the shelter there is a sign pointing to a rough track leading to St Piran's Church and Well. It also indicates St Nectan's Glen. You can also drive up this track about 250 m to a small car park by the church where the walk begins.

You can take the bus from Tintagel or Boscastle to the Rocky Valley Inn and walk up to the church.

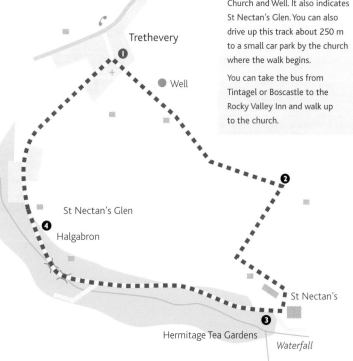

▲ Map: Explorer OL 28
▲ Distance: 15 km/9¼ miles
▲ Walk ID: 1428 Paul Edney

Difficulty rating

Time

▲ Hills or Fells, Pub, Church, Great Views, Café, Moor, Tea Shop, Ancient Monument

Grimspound from Widecombe

This walk from Widecombe takes in the Bronze Age enclosure at Grimspound, and includes spectacular views all along the top of Hameldown. The route also includes the remains of a medieval village.

1 From the car park, turn right along the path on the other side of the fence. Join the road on the other side of the village green. After 200 m turn left up the path signed Grimspound via Hameldown. Keep right and continue up a stony track. Go through the gate and take the path up the hillside.

2 The wall on your right turns right, where your path joins the Two Moors Way. Turn right and keep to the path just above the wall. Where the wall turns right again, head across open ground. Take either path to the top of Hameldown. Eventually, just to the left of the path, cross to the trig point at Hameldown Tor. Continue downhill towards Grimspound.

3 In the middle of the compound, turn right and follow the path towards the road at Natsworthy. Go through the gate onto the road, head left for 10 m, then turn right onto the bridle path. Go through the gate where the bridle path meets the road. Go past Jay's Grave, cross the road, and continue through the gate opposite onto the bridle path and over the hill.

4 Where the bridle path meets another road, with Bowerman's Nose to the left, turn right and follow the road towards Hound Tor.

5 At the crossroads, turn left and cross the grass to Hound Tor. Go down into

the remains of the medieval village. Pick up the path over the shoulder of the hill to the right of Greator Rocks. Go through the right-hand gate in the wall and take the right-hand path to Bonehill Down. At the top go through a gap in the wall and continue on the path downhill. Ignore the path to the left and continue to a gate.

6 Go through the gate and turn left onto the road, down to the river. Cross the cattle grid and head to the right, across the down. Take the left fork at the junction. Over the rise, Bell Tor is on your right.

7 Join the road and turn right, to reach a T-junction. Turn right to return to Widecombe.

further information

From the trig point at Hameldown Tor you have a bird's eye view of Grimspound, which is probably the best preserved Bronze Age enclosure on the moor.

Since 1860, when Kitty Jay's grave was discovered and restored, there have always been fresh flowers on the grave, although no one admits to putting them there.

Bowerman's Nose is only a few minutes off the route and is worth a visit. Legend has it that the shape is due to a bowman who discovered a coven of witches. They turned him and his hounds to stone. The hounds can be seen at Hound Tor.

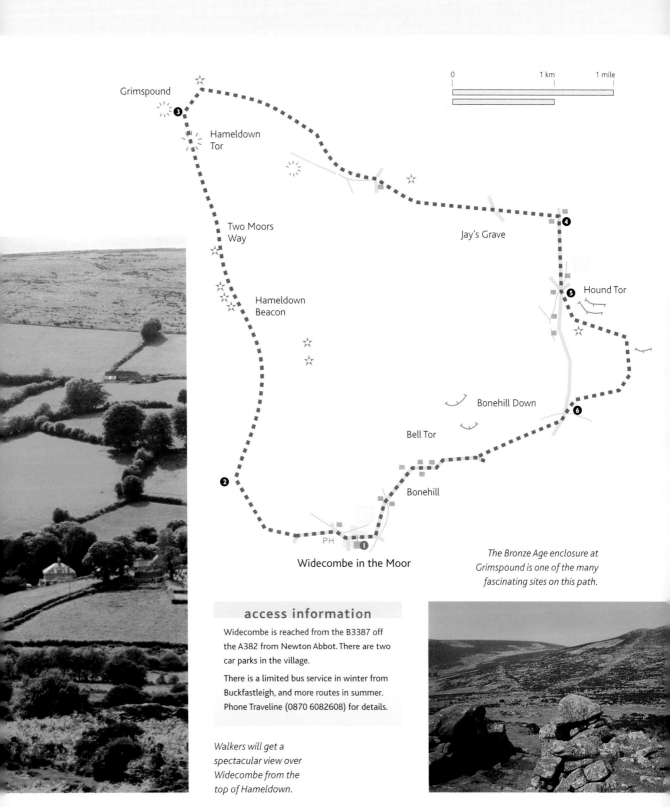

Grimspound

Hameldown
Tor

Two Moors
Way

Hameldown
Beacon

Jay's Grave

Hound Tor

Bonehill Down

Bell Tor

Bonehill

PH

Widecombe in the Moor

0   1 km   1 mile

*The Bronze Age enclosure at
Grimspound is one of the many
fascinating sites on this path.*

access information

Widecombe is reached from the B3387 off
the A382 from Newton Abbot. There are two
car parks in the village.

There is a limited bus service in winter from
Buckfastleigh, and more routes in summer.
Phone Traveline (0870 6082608) for details.

*Walkers will get a
spectacular view over
Widecombe from the
top of Hameldown.*

▲ Map: Explorer 28
▲ Distance: 4½ km/3 miles
▲ Walk ID: 1772 Dennis Blackford

Difficulty rating

Time

▲ Hills or Fells, Pub, Toilets, Church, Wildlife, Birds, Flowers, Great Views, Butterflies, Café, Gift Shop, Moorland, Restaurant, Tea Shop, Ancient Monument

Widecombe Circle

This is a wonderfully scenic walk, leading from Widecombe up to the open moor with its spectacular views over Hameldown, then on to the ancient stone remains at Wind Tor.

❶ Turn right out of the car park and walk across the green to the shops. Turn right again into Natsworthy Road (by the smaller car park). About 200 m along this road, you pass a small wooden bridge on your right. Take the turning on the left shortly afterwards, up a steep hill lined with beech trees. The path is signposted to Grimspound via Hameldown.

❷ At the top of the hill, where the road veers left through a gate, take the path that goes straight on. Continue up this path, then through the gate onto the open moor. The path takes you up over the moor, bearing slightly to the right, and parallel to a stone wall.

❸ Near the top of the hill, where the wall meets the track, you see a signpost pointing straight on. Walk on for a couple of metres until you come to a green path on your left, which almost doubles back on the way you have come. Take this path, bearing slightly to the right until you come to a road and small car parking space. Cross over the road and continue straight up the wide green track.

❹ At the split in the track, follow the fainter path to the right, towards Wind Tor. Spend some time exploring the Tor, then head east (follow your shadow on a sunny afternoon, or circle the Tor) until you can see the tower of Widecombe Church down in the valley.

❺ From here, head towards the 'V' of the valley, leading away to the left of Widecombe. There is no definite path: follow the sheep tracks in the rough direction. Further down the hillside, you come to a stone wall, with an established path running parallel alongside. Follow the path to the left, where it joins a wide track to the road.

❻ Turn right onto the road and head down Southcombe Hill. At the T-junction, turn left back into Widecombe.

further information

TAKE MOOR CARE: Bear in mind that the temperature up on the moor is likely to be much cooler than on lower ground. The weather can change very quickly so extra layers of clothing and a cagoule are highly recommended. Take some snacks and water in a rucksack together with a compass and map in case of mist or low cloud.

Wear stout walking boots to ensure your ankles and feet have sufficient support when walking on the unpredictable surface. Protect your legs from the gorse and heather by wearing trousers.

Sunshine lights the church tower in Widecombe village.

Park in the main car park opposite the
church between the 'Café on the Green' and
'The Wayside'. There is a small fee for
parking from Good Friday to 31 October;
parking is free at all other times, including
Sundays and bank holidays. There are toilets
at the car park entrance.

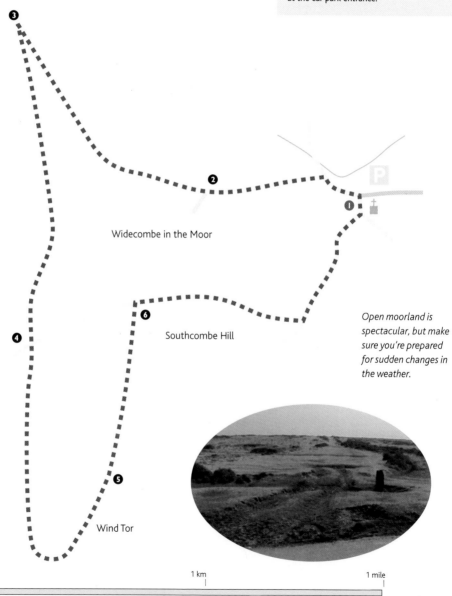

Widecombe in the Moor

Southcombe Hill

Wind Tor

*Open moorland is
spectacular, but make
sure you're prepared
for sudden changes in
the weather.*

0   1 km   1 mile

▲ Map: Explorer 102
▲ Distance: 7 km/4¼ miles
▲ Walk ID: 1038 Dennis Blackford

Difficulty rating

!!!

Time

● ● ●

▲ Hills or Fells, Lake/Loch, Wildlife, Birds, Flowers, Great Views, Butterflies, Industrial Archaeology, Moor, Ancient Monument

Nancledra

further information

From Roger's Tower there are fine views and you are surrounded by the ancient hill fort of Castle-an-Dinas.

This moorland walk to the ancient hill fort of Castle-an-Dinas and Roger's Tower, a folly built in 1798, offers superb views over St Michael's Mount and Penzance bay.

❶ Leave the car park and turn left down the main road to the junction. Turn right and continue up the country road.

❷ Cross a small bridge and turn left at a branch in the road. Look for a house called The Moors and take the farm track to the right of the house. Continue to the top of the hill.

❸ When you reach the junction, take the left-hand track until you come to a large house with a footpath to the right. Follow the path through a gate into a field. Cross the field to another gate in the top left-hand corner. Pass through the gate into another field and walk straight ahead to another gate leading into a large field.

❹ Cross the field to pass through a pair of gates, turn right onto the track and continue for about 800 m. At the chimney, turn left onto a wide track. Continue past an old engine house. After about 300 m turn right through a break in the wall. Turn left and follow the track round until it ends in a field near a pile of rocks. Cross the field diagonally right to reach a track leading to a gate with a stile. Cross the stile and turn left. Continue up to reach a wide track.

❺ Turn left and stay on the main track, which curves to the left at the new quarry. Go through the gate and walk along the quarry until you arrive at a path leading to Roger's Tower.

❻ After visiting the tower, return to the track along the quarry rim and turn left. The track goes through a gateway in a wall, becoming a rough path. At the end of the quarry, head downhill. Go through the gate and bear right across the moor. Continue across a telegraph pole on the ground, through a wide gap in the hedge and onto a farm track. Head to the right towards the farmhouse.

❼ Go through the gate by the farm and turn right, following the road to the main road. Turn left and walk back to the start.

access information

There is a bus service number 16 from St Ives and Penzance stopping in the village.

Nancledra is midway (about 6 km) on the B3311 road from St Ives to Penzance. On entering this small village watch for the tiny post office on the left. Turn up the track a little past the post office, which leads to the village car park.

St Michael's Mount, a former Benedictine priory and castle, is now the home of the St Aubyn family.

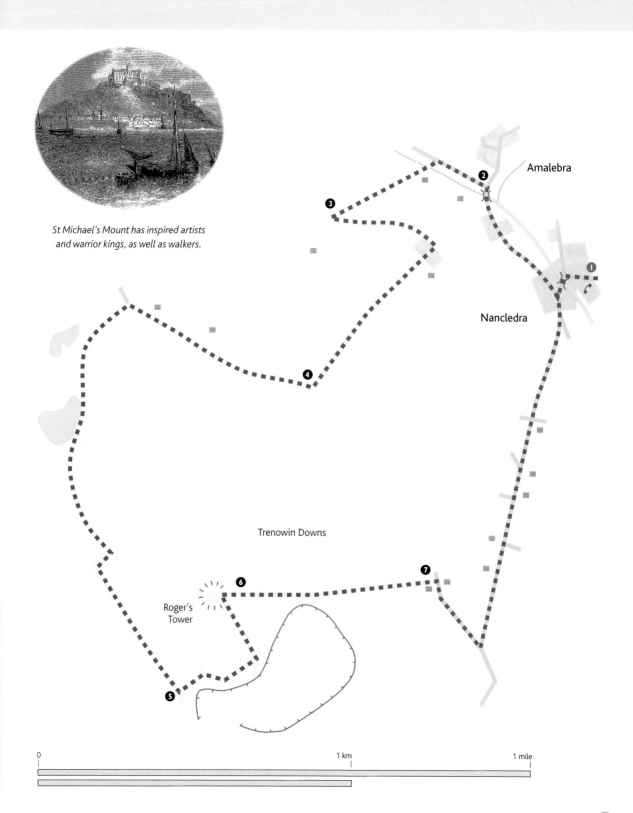

St Michael's Mount has inspired artists and warrior kings, as well as walkers.

Amalebra

Nancledra

Trenowin Downs

Roger's
Tower

0   1 km   1 mile

- ▲ Map: Explorer 190
- ▲ Distance: 2 km/1¼ miles
- ▲ Walk ID: 1686 Dennis Blackford

Difficulty rating

👣👣

Time

⬤

▲ Hills or Fells, River, Pub, Toilets, Museum, Birds, Flowers, Great Views, Butterflies, Café, Gift Shop, Food Shop, Restaurant, Tea Shop, Woodland

Camelford Town and River Camel

This pleasant walk follows an easy circuit through Camelford town, along the riverbank, then back through the fields of the Cornish countryside. It makes an ideal leisurely 'after lunch' stroll.

❶ Turn right out of the car park onto the main road. Walk down the hill, past Enfield Park on your right. Continue until you pass the old town hall, also on your right, then cross to the left-hand side of the road.

❷ Turn left under the second archway you come to, with 'The Moors' inscribed on a plaque above it. Walk down the slope onto the river path, bearing right. After a couple of hundred metres, the path turns sharp left across a footbridge and follows the river along the other bank. A second bridge returns you to the original bank shortly afterwards. Continue along the river path for about 1 km, passing through meadow and woodland. You go through several gates before reaching a road bridge.

❸ At the bridge, climb the short flight of slate steps up to the road and turn right. Climb the steep hill for about 200 m, until you reach the footpath on the right. Follow this marked path up the wooden steps into the meadow. Proceed, following the field boundary. The path swaps from left to right of the hedge several times.

❹ At the end of the last field, where the path runs along the right of the hedge, you pass through a gate onto Camelford's main road, opposite the police and ambulance stations. Turn right to walk back down into Camelford and to the north car park. To visit the cycling museum before doing so, turn left off the main road opposite the Co-op supermarket. This road also leads to the town's south car park.

access information

The walk starts from the car park at the Bude (north) end of town. Parking is free.

Camelford is accessible by bus or car.

Most of this leisurely stroll follows the footpath beside the River Camel.

further information

There are toilet facilities in Enfield Park, just down from the north car park.

Camelford's museum is devoted to the history of cycling. Its exhibits include 400 bikes, an old cycle repair shop, a collection of cycling medals and badges, and the first cycle oil lamp. Open Sundays to Thursdays, 10 a.m. to 5 p.m., all year round. For more details, telephone 01840 21281.

Camelford's old Town Hall has now been converted to house the local public library.

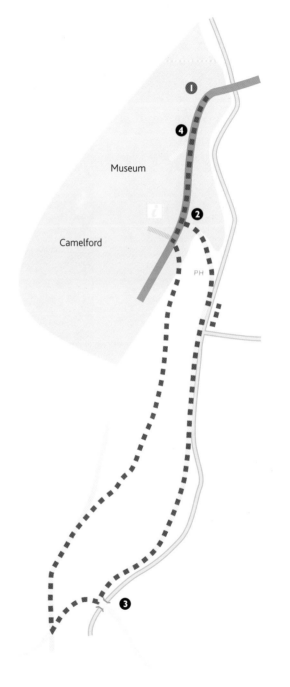

Museum

Camelford

PH

0   500 m   ½ mile

▲ Map: Explorer 54
▲ Distance: 11 km/6¾ miles
▲ Walk ID: 1266 Joy and Charles Boldero

Difficulty rating

Time

▲ River, Pub, Toilets, Play Area, Church, Wildlife, Birds, Flowers, Great Views, Butterflies, Food Shop

Puxton from Congresbury

This easy-going circuit is a chance to explore the moorland area of the Mendips, following country lanes and the old railway route known as the 'Strawberry Line'.

① Turn left out of the car park towards the river, then left again along the path signposted to Inwood. Continue along the path, keeping to the river. When you reach the weir, go through the gate and turn right over the bridge. At Weir Cottage, turn right again, then left at the T-junction that follows.

② On reaching the main road, cross over and turn left onto the pavement. You soon come to the Causeway, a 'No Through Road' on your right. Turn here and, where the path becomes a rough track, turn left and proceed with the football pitch on your right.

③ Turn right to cross the stile and the sports field beyond. Cross the bridge you come to on your left, then turn right along the ditch. Climb the stile and continue until you meet the old railway. Turn left onto the railway path and follow it to its end.

④ Turn right along the track at the end of the railway, then right again onto the country lane. Walk to Puxton, and turn left just after Apple Tree Cottage, crossing a bridge and a stile. Cross the meadow and the stile at the other end, and proceed through the churchyard.

further information

The 'Strawberry Line' is so called because the strawberries grown in this part of Somerset were transported by rail to the markets in London and the North. The line was closed in 1963. Nowadays the area is a nature reserve: look out for kingfishers along the riverbanks.

The name Congresbury is said to come from St Conger, a Celtic Missionary, who settled here in the 5th century. It is thought that the Romans had a wharf here behind where the Ship and Castle pub now stands. Goods would be loaded from the River Yeo onto carts. In the 15th century there was a market held in Broad Street and, until the 1900s, an annual fair was held here.

If you are very lucky, you may spot the electric-blue flash of a kingfisher on the banks of the River Yeo.

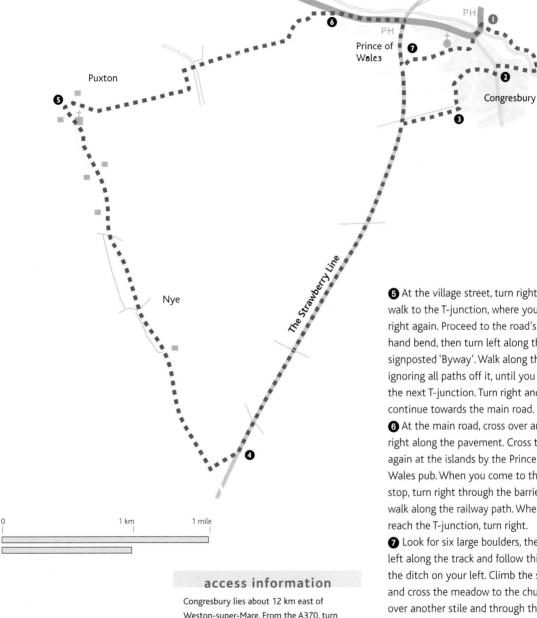

Puxton

⑤ Prince of Wales

Congresbury

PH

①

②

③

④

⑥

⑦

Nye

The Strawberry Line

0   1 km   1 mile

⑤ At the village street, turn right and walk to the T-junction, where you turn right again. Proceed to the road's right-hand bend, then turn left along the track signposted 'Byway'. Walk along the path, ignoring all paths off it, until you reach the next T-junction. Turn right and continue towards the main road.

⑥ At the main road, cross over and turn right along the pavement. Cross the road again at the islands by the Prince of Wales pub. When you come to the bus stop, turn right through the barrier and walk along the railway path. When you reach the T-junction, turn right.

⑦ Look for six large boulders, then turn left along the track and follow this with the ditch on your left. Climb the stile, and cross the meadow to the church, over another stile and through the churchyard. Continue along Paul's Causeway for a moment, before turning left along the narrow shopping street. At the end of the street by the traffic lights, cross the road and walk back over the bridge to the walk's start.

access information

Congresbury lies about 12 km east of Weston-super-Mare. From the A370, turn off at Kent Road. The walk begins at Congresbury car park behind the bus stop and river bridge at the Millennium Green. For details of bus services, telephone 0800 260 250.

▲ Map: Explorer 140
▲ Distance: 10 km/6¼ miles
▲ Walk ID: 1306 John Thorn

Difficulty rating

Time

▲ Hills or Fells, River, Wildlife, Birds, Flowers, Great Views, Butterflies, Public Transport, Woodland

Holford and the Quantocks

This circular route follows Holford Combe up to the ridge of the Quantocks. From Thorncombe Hill you get a great view of the coast of South Wales at Aberthaw, with the tops of the Brecon Beacons on your right, and Exmoor, the Brendon Hills and the vale of Taunton Deane on your left.

❶ From the car park, walk back down to the road, bearing right. When you come to a bridge over a stream, bear right past the thatched cottage; follow the gravel path round to your left then turn right onto the road signposted to Holford Combe. Follow the road past the hotel, then continue straight ahead, following the bridleway signs. The path divides and rejoins several times along the combe. It doesn't matter which path you take as long as you stay at the bottom.

❷ Walk on until you reach a glade where the valley divides. Rather than follow one of the streams, take the wide grassy path that runs straight ahead. This becomes stony as you climb up through a shallow valley and onto open hillside.

❸ As you reach the crest of the hill, you come to a junction of several paths. Take the stony track to the right that you can see running along the flank of the hill. Turn round first for a view of Steep Holm in the Bristol Channel. Continue on the track, ignoring the track that you come to that leads off to the right. The large structures you can see over your right shoulder are the Hinkley Point nuclear power stations. As you round the shoulder of the hill you can see Dunkery Beacon, the highest point of Exmoor, ahead.

❹ Bear right onto the wide, well-worn track. Directly ahead, before you turn, is a view of the Brendon Hills. Walk up the rise, then take the grassy track ahead to the top of the hill, ignoring the track signposted for 'motor vehicles'. Continue to the top of Thorncombe Hill and then walk on to join the 'motor vehicles' track further along.

❺ The path soon drops down into Hodder's Combe on your right. Take this path, following the combe downstream for about 2 km until you are back at the starting point.

access information

The walk starts in the car park in Holford village. Turn off the main road and follow the wooden car-park signs.

A bus service from Bridgwater to Minehead stops nearby.

The climb to the top of Thorncombe Hill is rewarded by the all-round view once you reach the summit.

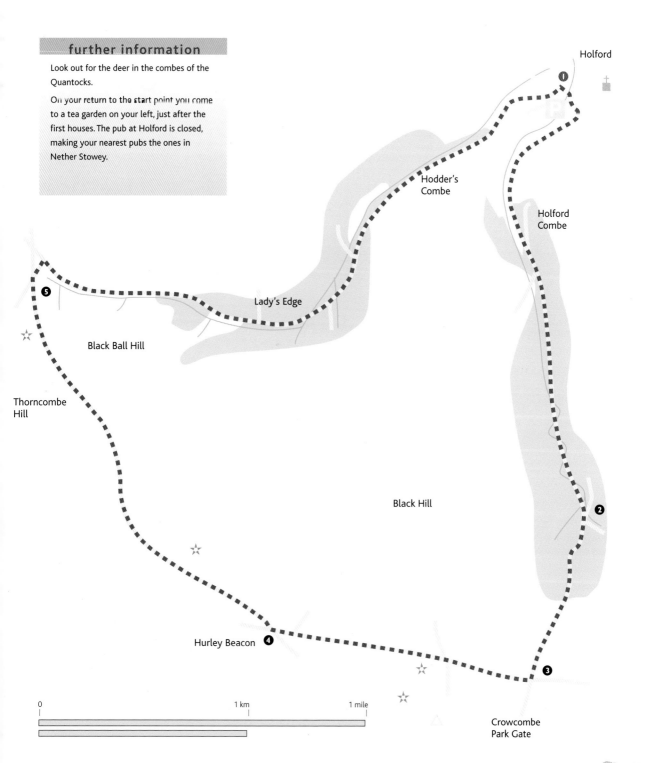

Holford

Hodder's Combe

Holford Combe

Lady's Edge

⑤

Black Ball Hill

Thorncombe Hill

Black Hill

②

Hurley Beacon ④

③

0   1 km   1 mile

Crowcombe Park Gate

▲ Map: Explorer 141
▲ Distance: 10 km/6¼ miles
▲ Walk ID: 1080 Tony Brotherton

Difficulty rating

Time

▲ Hills or Fells, National Trust/NTS, Wildlife, Birds, Flowers, Great Views, Butterflies

Black Down from Charterhouse

From the Roman lead-mining centre around the isolated Mendip hamlet of Charterhouse, this bracing upland walk crosses Black Down with its immense views and returns via dry limestone valleys and Velvet Bottom Nature Reserve.

❶ Turn right out of the car park onto the road. Walk to the minor crossroads and take the unsigned lane to the right, proceeding to the small parking area and information board on Roman lead mines.
❷ Take the path to your left and go left again at the fork that follows (not to Nordrach). Walk along the gravel path to the signpost, then turn left onto the narrow path to walk through the old lead workings, skirt the reed pond on the left and cross a stile. Follow the stone wall from here, climbing to the road. At the road, turn right and walk until you reach the 'No Through Road' sign.
❸ Take this left turn and climb the bridleway up to the radio station, then turn left and follow the track. You eventually reach a gate by a cluster of trees in a hollow. Pass through the gate and proceed straight ahead on the path across Black Down to the triangulation pillar at Beacon Batch, 325 m above sea level.
❹ From the pillar, continue on the path across the moor. At the wide crossing track, turn left and proceed to the gate, then head downhill to the road at Tyning's Farm and Trekking Centre. Turn left onto the road and walk to the entrance of Piney Sleight and Charterhouse Farm.
❺ Walk down the farm drive until just before Charterhouse Farm, then turn

right to cross the cattle grids. At the top of the rise, before a further grid, turn left onto the field path marked 'Cheddar 3'. Continue on the path, keeping straight ahead at the stile and woods. At the bottom of your steep descent, you come to a kissing gate.

❻ Pass through the gate to enter Black Rock Valley and continue until you reach a second gate on your left, before a National Trust sign. Pass through this gate to enter Velvet Bottom Nature Reserve. Eventually the path reaches the road, where you turn left to reach the church and return to the car park at Charterhouse.

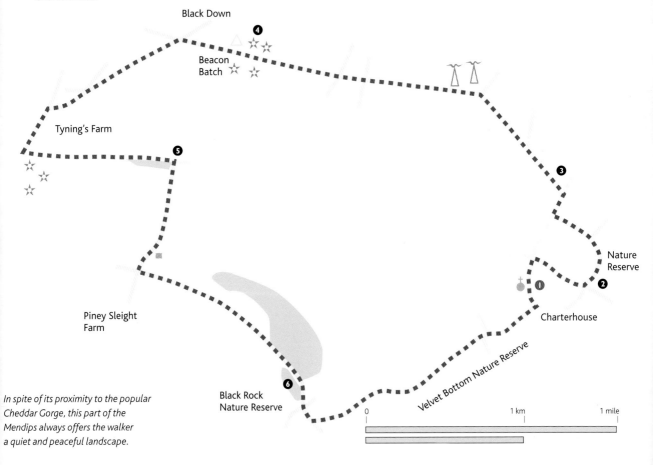

In spite of its proximity to the popular Cheddar Gorge, this part of the Mendips always offers the walker a quiet and peaceful landscape.

▲ Map: Explorer OL 22
▲ Distance: 6 km/3¾ miles
▲ Walk ID: 719 Peter Salenieks

Difficulty rating

Time

▲ Sea, Toilets, Wildlife, Birds, Great Views

Hengistbury Head

The route of this popular walk takes in historic Hengistbury Head, a nature reserve and the beach at Sandspit. There are lovely views over Christchurch Harbour and across to the Isle of Wight.

❶ Start with the Ranger Office and Land Train terminus behind you and walk about 50 m along the road until you reach a junction with the track just before the Double Dykes. Bear right and go along the track. At end of the Double Dykes turn left and follow a path that goes along the cliff top heading towards Hengistbury Head. Continue past Barn Field and two paths on your left. Climb steadily, keeping the wildlife pond on your right, to reach the top of Warren Hill. Walk along a gravel track, past the coastguard lookout station and, later, a junction on the left.

❷ At the crossroads turn right and follow the track along the cliff top, passing the southern end of the wildlife pond in the old quarry on your left. Follow the track to the southern tip of Hengistbury Head, before turning left to reach broad steps that lead down to the beach.

further information

Hengistbury Head has witnessed 11,000 years of human history, including a Stone Age camp on Warren Hill, an Iron Age port and 18th-century quarrying. Today it is a popular tourist spot, including a nature reserve, which is home to a variety of birds, insects and small mammals.

Hengistbury Head is a magnificent setting for a footpath. It has a variety of wildlife as well as a wealth of ancient archaeological sites.

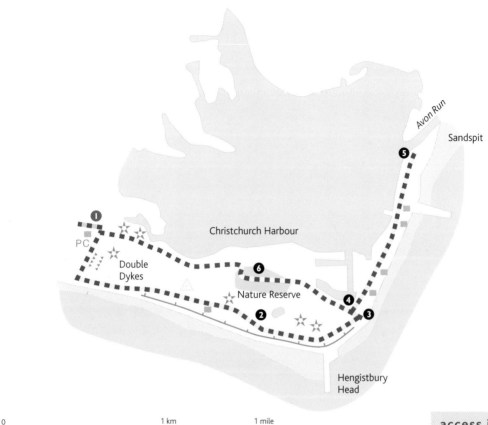

Avon Run

Sandspit

5

Christchurch Harbour

1

P C

Double
Dykes

6

Nature Reserve

2

4

3

Hengistbury
Head

0   1 km   1 mile

3 Descend the steps and bear left to pick up a broad path, which leads inland from the beach huts at Sandspit, until you reach the road.

4 Turn right and follow the road towards Sandspit. Pass the Land Train terminus and the pontoon for the ferry to Mudeford Quay on your left. When you reach the Hut Café, cross between it and the beach office to reach the seaward side of Sandspit and walk towards the end of the spit, where Avon Run marks the outflow from Christchurch Harbour into the sea.

5 Retrace your route from Avon Run and head right along the road, passing Holloway's Dock, which is a Site of Special Scientific Interest, on your right. Pass a track on your left before entering woodland. Continue until you see a wooded track on your left which leads gently uphill.

6 Follow the track about 50 m uphill for an optional detour to the wildlife pond, then go back to the road to return to your starting point.

access information

Cars can be parked in Hengistbury Head car park. This is approached from the A35, turning south onto the B3059 and then east onto the Broadway to the west of Tuckton.

Hengistbury Head is also accessible by bus during the summer. Open Top Coastal Service 12 runs between Sandbanks and Christchurch Quay from the end of May to the end of September. Telephone Yellow Buses (01202) 636060 for further information or visit www.yellowbuses.co.uk.

▲ Map: Explorer 15
▲ Distance: 5 km/3 miles
▲ Walk ID: 2079 David Stewart

Difficulty rating

Time

▲ Sea, Museum, Church, Great Views,
Butterflies, Ancient Monument

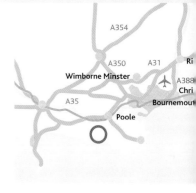

Worbarrow Beach and Tyneham

This short but arduous route begins high above the Dorset coast at Lulworth and makes a sharp descent to the popular Worbarrow Bay, before returning via the village of Tyneham.

1 Take the Lulworth Range path from the car park. You are only allowed to walk along paths with yellow marker posts. At the flagpole, continue straight on along the top of the high ridge. You have a great view of Lulworth Castle to your right, and the sea on your left.

2 Bear left off the track onto a grassy path, following the marker posts. Walk to Flower's Barrow Iron Age hill fort and then turn sharp left through a gap in the embankments. Climb the stile, marked as the Hardy Way, and make the steep descent. Continue on the coastal path to the beach, a good place for a picnic.

This walk is perfect for observing the beauty of the Dorset coastline, including Lulworth Cove, below.

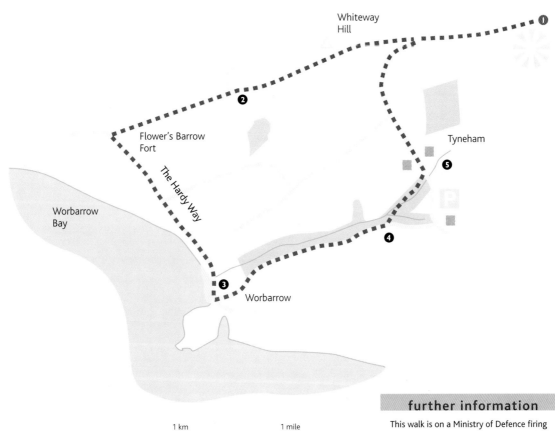

Whiteway
Hill

❷

Flower's Barrow
Fort

Tyneham

❺

The Hardy Way

Worbarrow
Bay

❹

❸

Worbarrow

0   1 km   1 mile

access information

The walk starts at the car park at Whiteway viewpoint. Take the A351 from Wareham or Swanage and follow signs to East Lulworth and Tyneham.

❸ Turn left off the coastal path, away from the beach, and proceed uphill along the well-established track.

❹ Turn left into the woods towards Tyneham. Once through the woods, keep to the left and you come to the village pond.

❺ The track back to the car park is just behind the church, indicated by yellow marker posts. Climb uphill along the track until you reach the flagpole. Turn right to retrace your steps back to the start point.

further information

This walk is on a Ministry of Defence firing range which is sometimes closed to the public, although it is usually open at weekends. The MOD road to the viewpoint and Tyneham can also be closed at these times.

This route is not recommended during or after rain as the steep, grassy descent from Flower's Barrow to Worbarrow Bay can be dangerous.

For an alternative route, leave your car at Tyneham village, and turn left when you reach the flagpole, proceeding to waymark 2. The advantage of this is that most of the climbing is done at the start of the walk.

▲ Map: Explorer OL 15
▲ Distance: 15 km/9¼ miles
▲ Walk ID: 389 Al Rodger

Difficulty rating

Time

▲ Hills or Fells, Sea, Pub, Toilets, Wildlife, Great Views

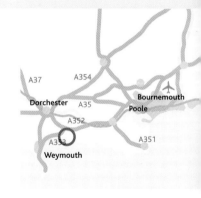

Lulworth and White Nothe Coastal Tour

Starting on the ridge above Ringstead, the route first crosses downland to West Lulworth and the magnificent coast at Lulworth Cove and Durdle Door, to return along the cliff-top path.

❶ Exit the car park over the stile at the far end and continue down the track. Where the track bears sharp right, cross the stile and continue up the track. Keep straight ahead through two more stiles and a gate.

❷ At the second gate, keep straight ahead over the next two rises. As the path rises for a third time, turn right over the stile at the signpost to Newlands Farm Camp Site. Go through Newlands Farm and continue past West Lulworth Church and down to Lulworth Cove.

❸ The walk resumes from the pay-and-display car park up Hambury Tout on the stone path, dropping down to the cliff above Durdle Door, then over the small hill to Scratchy Bottom.

❹ From Scratchy Bottom cross the stile at the foot of Swyre Head and follow the path diagonally uphill. Cross the stile at the top, to reach a well-used path. Follow the path until reaching the obelisk.

❺ At the obelisk, take one of the paths round the hillside and over the summit to the coastguard cottages at White Nothe. Continue along the cliff top, with Weymouth Bay in sight ahead. Cross the stile and descend the field onto a track at the next stile.

❻ Follow the track uphill, bearing left at a post box. Continue ahead to the car park.

The stretch of coastline between Durdle Door and Lulworth Cove is possibly the most impressive in the whole of Dorset.

access information

This walk starts from the Ringstead Bay National Trust car park on the ridge above Ringstead. Take the Ringstead turning off the A353 between Poxwell and Osmington. Follow the road ahead to the car park, parking towards the far end.

No practical access by public transport.

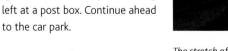

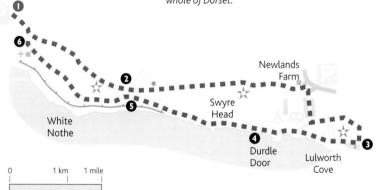

▲ Map: Explorer 102
▲ Distance: 6½ km/4 miles
▲ Walk ID: 124 Colin Ward

Difficulty rating

Time

▲ Sea, Pub, Great Views

Lamorna Cove from Mousehole

This walk takes you from the picturesque fishing village of Mousehole to Lamorna, returning along the South West Coast Path.

❶ From the harbour, take the lane past the Lobster Pot restaurant to the Methodist chapel. Walk up the hill, out of the village, to the point where it bears to the right. Keep on the road for about 100 m, and follow the footpath sign to take a path on the left.

❷ Turn right into the field and walk round the edge, until you reach the stile on the far side. Continue walking across the field to reach the farm at Kemyel Drea. The path passes to the right of the first building, and then between the large sheds. Once through the farm, follow the hedge and pick up the path that leads into the hedges beyond.

❸ Walk to the stile and turn left. Continue straight up the lane past the farmhouses, and the gate marked with a Caravan Club sign. Cross the stile, and continue across the fields to the farmhouses of Kemyel Wartha. Follow the track through the hamlet, as it bears right to the footpath sign. Take the path on the left down to the quarry. Continue past the quarry to Lamorna Cove.

❹ Take the obvious path up to Carn-du and continue round the coast for 3 km. Eventually you will come to the road, where you should continue straight on, and down into Mousehole.

further information

The disused quarry on the way to Lamorna Cove supplied the stone for London Bridge. The cove was once used for shipping the stone, but the difficult task of navigating the harbour rendered it redundant in the last century.

The South West Coast Path goes through a small wooded nature reserve.

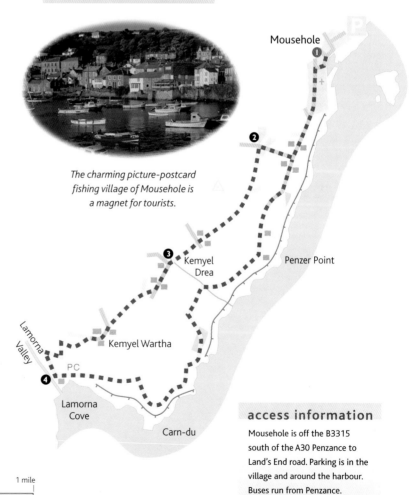

The charming picture-postcard fishing village of Mousehole is a magnet for tourists.

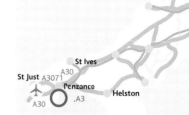

access information

Mousehole is off the B3315 south of the A30 Penzance to Land's End road. Parking is in the village and around the harbour. Buses run from Penzance.

0   1 km   1 mile

▲ Map: Explorer OL 15
▲ Distance: 10 km/6¼ miles
▲ Walk ID: 365 Al Rodger

Difficulty rating

Time

▲ Sea, Toilets, Church, National Trust, Wildlife, Birds, Flowers, Great Views

Old Harry and Ballard Down from Studland

A circular walk from Studland to Old Harry passing Studland's Norman church en route. Continuing up the coast and along the top of Ballard Down, the route returns to Studland via Agglestone Rock.

❶ Exit the car park away from the beach, immediately turning left at the road junction past the car park sign. Turn right at the road junction by the Manor House Hotel. Turn left through the gate and follow the path past St Nicholas's Church and continue straight ahead to the marker post. Turn left down the road and where the road bends left, continue up the track straight ahead to the right of the public toilets. Keep straight ahead to Old Harry, where tracks join at a marker stone.

❷ The route continues up the cliff path. Keep outside the fenced area ahead and pause to sample the views behind you. Continue along the South West Coast Path. Keep left at the marker stone, taking in the superior views as you go.

❸ At the fence line coming in from the right, bear right away from the cliff and go through the gate and gap in the ancient dyke. Continue along the crest of Ballard Down.

❹ At the obelisk, continue straight ahead through the gate and down the track that bends to the right down to the road. Turn left down the road. Take the path on the right. Go over two stiles and through the woods, straight over the golf course to reach the stile onto the road.

access information

Studland is on the B3351 east of the A351. The walk starts from Middle Beach car park, situated at the end of Beach Road, the northern of the two side roads heading towards the beach.

A bus runs hourly from Bournemouth to Swanage over the ferry and stops at the end of Beach Road.

This chalk arch and stack form a spectacular view at the heart of Studland Bay.

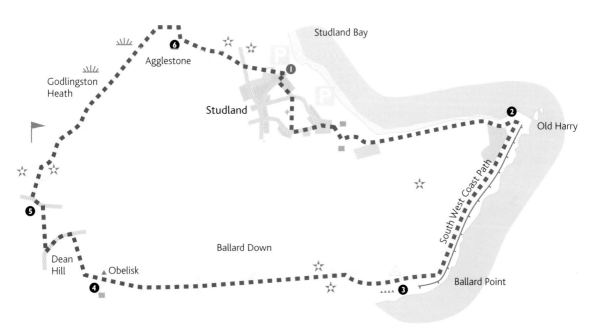

The Agglestone Rock
(composed of sandstone
in an area of limestone)
is said to have been thrown
by the Devil from the Isle
of Wight at Corfe Castle.

further information

St Nicholas's Church has been described as 'the most exciting building in Purbeck'. It is Norman, built on the remnants of a Saxon church destroyed by the Danes.

Old Harry is the large stack at the end of The Foreland. Sea birds abound at The Foreland, as do land species in the nature reserve on the cliff top. The spot with its views was special enough for the author H.G. Wells to have his ashes scattered here.

The obelisk at point 4 was brought to Swanage from London as ship's ballast. It was positioned on top of the Bronze Age barrow to commemorate the first piped water supply into Swanage.

Legend has it that Agglestone Rock was thrown here from the Isle of Wight by the Devil, who was aiming at Old Harry or Corfe Castle.

5 Meander left and then right. Pass through two gates onto the good path. Keep straight ahead at the first two marker stones making for Agglestone Studland Heath. Turn left onto a bridle path just before the 'No Entry' signs, skirting the edge of the golf course. At the gate continue straight ahead on towards Agglestone. From Agglestone, the route continues down into the valley, ascending the far side before bearing right and descending again. At the main track, turn right downhill. The track turns sharply to the right and crosses a ford.

6 Continue up the track and through the gate, turning right at the main road. Cross the road and follow the path on the left through the gully to Beach Road. Turn left to return to the car park.

Osmington and Ringstead

▲ Map: Explorer 15
▲ Distance: 12 km/7½ miles
▲ Walk ID: 2078 David Stewart

Difficulty rating

Time

▲ Sea, Pub, Toilets, Play Area, National Trust/NTS, Birds, Great Views, Butterflies, Café, Good for Kids

This is an enjoyable, family-friendly walk covering a delightful stretch of the Dorset coast and surrounding countryside.

❶ Come out through the car park entrance and walk back along the road for about 1 km. Take the footpath on the right and walk downhill. Follow the track through the farm and uphill again until you emerge at the A352.

❷ Cross the road to the footpath directly opposite and proceed uphill. Further on the path crosses a field and is harder to follow – head to the left of the mobile phone mast. Pass through the gate at the bottom and cross the track from Poxwell Manor (on your right). Walk up towards the mast, following the sign for the Hardy Way. Once at the mast, veer to the left and follow the ancient trackway to White Horse Hill.

❸ Just short of the summit and the gated stile, there is a left turn signposted to Osmington. Follow this stony track downhill to the village. Turn round on your way down to admire the White Horse on the hillside behind you.

❹ At Osmington, turn left onto Village Street, which is signposted to Osmington Mills. The street bends sharply to the right before joining the main road at the Sun Ray pub. Turn left onto the road and walk for about 125 m before crossing. Proceed along the footpath by the cottage. When you reach the stile by the busy dairy farm, cross over and go through the gate opposite. (If the farmer is moving cattle

The White Horse, cut into the turf to reveal the chalk, at White Horse Hill.

the path may appear barred.) Follow the path as it veers to the left until you emerge into an open field.

❺ Make your way to the field boundary by the campsite. Follow the hedge to the far corner and climb the stile to join the coast path. Walk along the boards through the trees to the quiet road. Turn right and walk for a couple of hundred metres to the Smuggler's Inn.

❻ Walk round the left-hand side of the pub to find the coastal path. Pass through the kissing gate by the white house and then on up to the next kissing gate to follow the coastal path to Ringstead, where the path veers inland.

access information

The walk begins at the South Down car park at Ringstead, just off the A352 east of Weymouth.

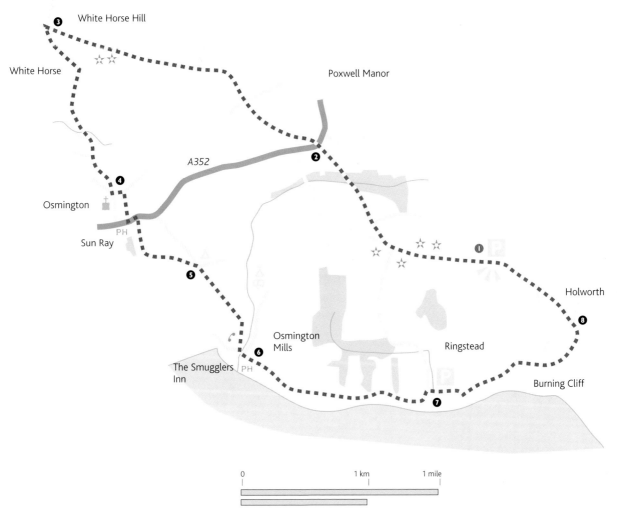

White Horse Hill

White Horse

Poxwell Manor

A352

Osmington

Sun Ray

Osmington
Mills

Ringstead

Holworth

The Smugglers
Inn

Burning Cliff

0   1 km   1 mile

7 As you come up to the car park, take the right-hand turn for the coastal path, signposted to White Nothe. After a while, cross the stile on the right, walk through the meadow to the beach and walk along to the steps, at the top of which you rejoin the coastal path at Burning Cliff. Continue on the coastal path to Holworth, climbing steadily and veering left.

8 Where the track forks, keep to the left and head back to your car.

▲ Map: Explorer 110
▲ Distance: 6 km/3¾ miles
▲ Walk ID: 1829 Dennis Blackford

Difficulty rating

Time

▲ Sea, Toilets, Wildlife, Birds, Flowers, Great Views, Butterflies, Café, Gift Shop, Public Transport, Restaurant, Tea Shop, Woodland

Anstey's Cove from Kent's Cavern

This walk is known as the Bishop's Walk because it was created by the Bishop of Exeter in 1840 as a health-enhancing opportunity for 'quiet repose'. There are several detour points along the way, offering stunning views and interesting places to explore.

1 Take the path from the car park past the shop and toilets. Walk down the steps and follow the woodland path as far as the house on the left. On reaching the junction, take the left-hand path signposted 'Meadfoot Beach'. Follow this path down, then along the edge of the woodland.

2 At the bottom of the hill, follow a second signpost to Meadfoot Beach left through the metal gate, or continue up the path into the woods, bearing left at the junction. The latter brings you out further along the beach.

3 When you reach the road, cross over to the car park on Meadfoot esplanade. You can wander from here along the sea front, and to the refreshment facilities and toilets at the other end. To continue the walk, follow the small path up the hillside, which is on the left-hand side of the car park as you face the sea. Turn right at the top and follow the road (Ilsham Marine Drive) along the cliff top.

4 About 600 m along the road, you come to some gardens on your right. Immediately before the gardens, there is a path leading towards the sea. You can either take this path or continue along the road past the gardens.

5 Opposite the mass of Thatchers' Rock, the coast path ends in a grassy area. Go through the opening in the bank into the gardens – a good spot for

a picnic – then walk up the right-hand side of the gardens back to the road.

6 Another 500 m brings you to a road on your left called Thatcher Avenue. At this point, you can take another optional detour through the metal gate on your right down to Hope's Nose, an area of Special Scientific Interest. This is another ideal stopping-off point for a picnic lunch. Once back on the route proper, continue along the Marine Drive for another 700 m until you enter a built-up area.

Much of this walk takes you along broad woodland paths.

further information

The complex of caves at Kent's Cavern are the oldest recognizable human dwellings in Britain, dating back some two million years to the Palaeolithic period. The site is now a popular tourist attraction, with a visitor centre and good facilities.

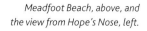

Meadfoot Beach, above, and the view from Hope's Nose, left.

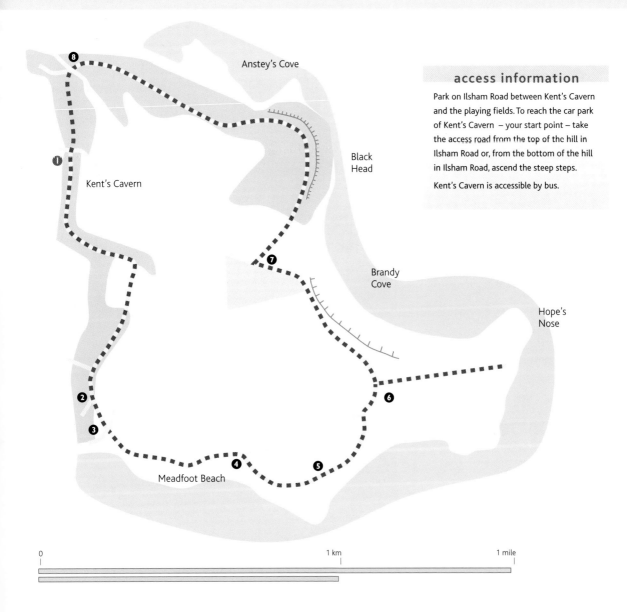

Anstey's Cove

Black
Head

Kent's Cavern

Brandy
Cove

Hope's
Nose

Meadfoot Beach

access information

Park on Ilsham Road between Kent's Cavern
and the playing fields. To reach the car park
of Kent's Cavern – your start point – take
the access road from the top of the hill in
Ilsham Road or, from the bottom of the hill
in Ilsham Road, ascend the steep steps.

Kent's Cavern is accessible by bus.

0   1 km   1 mile

❼ Just past the first house on your left,
there is a small access road. Follow this
road round to the left before going
through a metal gate and rejoining the
coast path. Proceed along the coast
path past Brandy Cove – named for its
smuggling past – and into more
woodland. Continue straight on, ignoring
the path to the right when you come to

the junction. Walk a little further on,
and you can see Anstey's Cove below.
❽ To explore the cove, take the path
down to your right when you reach the
road. Otherwise cross the road and enter
the playing fields. Walk diagonally across,
towards the roof of the players' changing
rooms in the distance. Just beyond this
building turn right into Ilsham Road.

▲ Map: Explorer OL 20
▲ Distance: 5 km/3 miles
▲ Walk ID: 1131 Dennis Blackford

Difficulty rating

Time

▲ Hills or Fells, Sea, National Trust/ NTS, Wildlife, Birds, Flowers, Great Views, Butterflies, Public Transport

Man Sands from Sharkham Head

This is an easy-to-follow circular walk that passes along tracks and quiet Devonshire country lanes to Man Sands before returning to Sharkham Head along the beautiful South West Coast Path.

1 From the far end of the car park, cross the stile and follow the grit track. After about 100 m, at the first bend, take the path off to the right. Follow the path through a pair of stone gateposts (it can be muddy at times).

2 At the end of the path, turn right and follow the farm track.

3 The track exits into a country road through South Bay Holiday Camp before joining the road to the car park. Turn left onto the road for about 50 m and, immediately past the entrance to the holiday camp, go up the path to the right of the wall. The path widens to become a farm track. Follow the track uphill until arriving at a T-junction. Turn left.

4 The track ends at a country road. Turn left to follow the road. After about 800 m, the road ends at Southdown Barns. To the left of the gates to a large house, join a wooded lane leading downhill to Man Sands. About 500 m down, where the lane bends to the right, continue on down the smaller path off the bend.

5 The path now leads out on the grass area above the beach. After spending time at the beach, take the coast path up the steep hill to the left.

Sharkham Head is a Site of Special Scientific Interest.

6 After about 2 km the path goes over a stone stile into a field. Continue along the coast side of the field. At the end of the field, go over the wooden stile and turn left through the gap, which will lead back to the car park.

access information

From Brixham town centre, go up Bolton Street and, just past the traffic lights, turn left into Castor Road and follow to the top. Turn left into St Mary's Road, which will take you to the car park.

There is a bus service to South Bay Holiday Camp and the walk can be started and finished here.

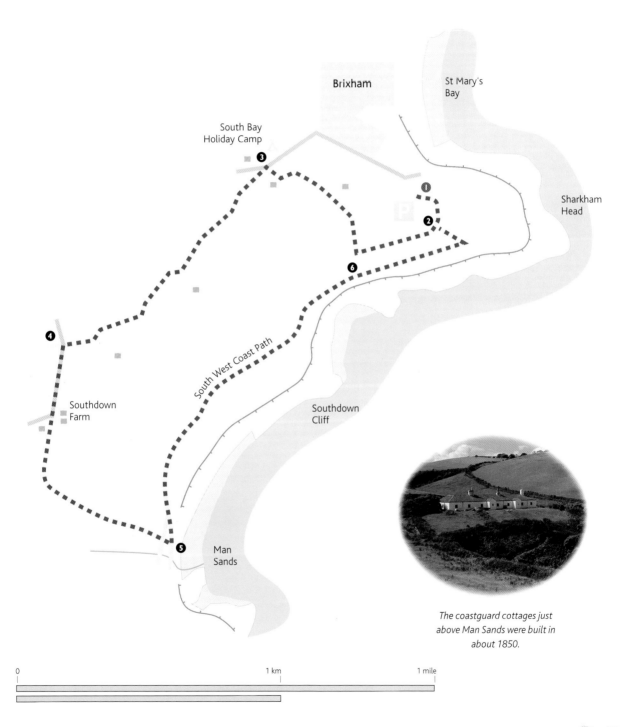

Brixham

St Mary's
Bay

Sharkham
Head

South Bay
Holiday Camp

3

1

2

6

4

South West Coast Path

Southdown
Farm

Southdown
Cliff

5

Man
Sands

*The coastguard cottages just
above Man Sands were built in
about 1850.*

0   1 km   1 mile

▲ Map: Explorer OL 20
▲ Distance: 4 km/2½ miles
▲ Walk ID: 995 Dennis Blackford

Difficulty rating

Time

▲ Hills or Fells, Sea, Wildlife, Birds,
Flowers, Great Views, Butterflies,
Industrial Archaeology

Scabbacombe Coast – Two Bays Walk

This is another pleasant walk taking in part of the South West Coast Path and visiting the two bays of Man Sands and Scabbacombe Sands. It is a fairly short walk, so you will have plenty of time to relax on the beach if you wish.

1 Leave the car park and turn right into the road. Follow the road down about 1 km to Man Sands car park. Continue past Man Sands car park. The tarmac road now continues as a stony track. As you near the beach, the path branches to the right. Continue straight on to Man Sands Beach. Return to the branch and walk up a side-shoot for about 100 m to reach a stile on your right. The stone structure that you pass on the way to the beach is an old limekiln where lime was baked to make fertilizer.

2 Go into the field via the stile. The path is clearly signposted and passes behind the old coastguard cottages. Walk up the path and through the gap in the wall.

3 Take the path up the hill to the top of the field. Walk south along the South West Coast Path, bearing around to your right and along to the gate.

4 Pass through the gate or over the stile and follow the coast path for about another kilometre to reach another gate and stile.

5 After passing through the gate, continue along the coast path for about 400 m until you come to a stile over the fence, leading to Scabbacombe Beach. After spending some time on the beach, return up the path to the stile. Walk back along the coast about 200 m and slightly up to the left, until you come to an isolated stile with no fence. Turn left here and follow the sheep path to the main gate leading into the farm track.

6 Pass through the gate or over the stile onto the farm track. At the top of the farm track, pass the large gate and go through the kissing gate back to the car park.

access information

By car, take the Brixham to Kingswear road. About 1.5 km from the small roundabout, halfway down a hill past the holiday camp, turn left, signposted 'Kingston, Boohay, Woodhuish and Brownstone'. After about 1.5 km, this lane branches into two lanes with dead-end signs. Take the left-hand one. Just under 1 km away, an opening in the hedgerow on the right leads into the car park.

By bus, take the Brixham to Kingswear bus to the end of the above lane. It is about 2 km from the bus stop to the car park.

further information

The left-hand end of Scabbacombe is a 'clothes optional' beach.

The rugged coastline between Brixham and Scabbacombe.

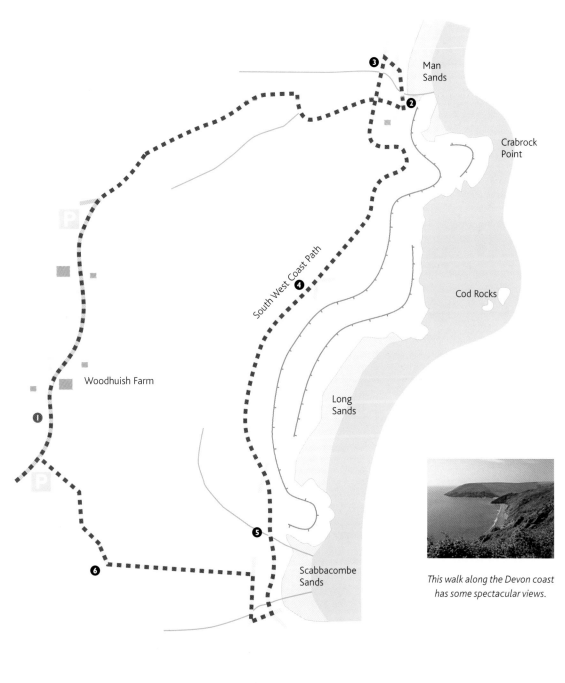

3

Man
Sands

2

Crabrock
Point

South West Coast Path

4

Cod Rocks

P

P

Woodhuish Farm

1

Long
Sands

5

6

Scabbacombe
Sands

*This walk along the Devon coast
has some spectacular views.*

0   1 km   1 mile

▲ Map: Explorer 20

▲ Distance: 10 km/6¼ miles

▲ Walk ID: 2061 Dave Pawley

Difficulty rating

Time

▲ River, Sea, Great Views

River Erme and St Anchorite's Rock from Battisborough Cross

This walk takes you along a scenic stretch of the South West Coast Path from the mouth of the River Erme along to west of St Anchorite's Rock. The well-signed path leads you onto and above secluded coves, a rocky headland and grassy cliff top.

❶ Take the turning signposted to Mothecombe and follow the road downhill, passing under a bridge and then a car park on your left until you get close to sea level and reach a signpost for Mothecombe Slipway. For a good view of the River Erme out to sea, turn down left to Mothecombe Beach.

❷ Back at the signpost, go through the kissing gate and follow the path as it climbs up and over a wooded headland. There is a viewing point at the top. Descend down steep steps through the wood until you come to the popular Meadowsfoot Beach.

❸ Walk across the beach to the old roundhouse at the far end and make your way up the steps and back onto the coastal path. Follow the path as it climbs up and sweeps round a broad expanse of headland. After the initial climb, the going is relatively easy.

❹ At Bugle Hole, the path takes you down steeply to cross over a stream, then swings out and round another headland. Follow the marked path as it climbs steadily up to the well-known landmark of St Anchorite's Rock, visible for miles out to sea. You are approaching a steep section, so you may want to break here to enjoy the views.

❺ Continue west from the rock and walk down into the valley, then up the other side to cross the gate and stile. Soon afterwards, the path swings sharp right up a short, steep hill, across a stile and then on up to a further stile, with a farmer's warning notice to the right. Climb the stile and follow the path across a grassy area for about 350 m until you reach yet another stile, with a gate alongside. The headland below you is Blackaterry Point.

access information

Park at Battisborough Cross, where the walk begins.

Although the beaches around the Erme are part of the Flete Estate and therefore open only at specific times, the South West Coast Path is a public right of way and, providing you keep to it, you are allowed to cross the beaches at any time.

Bugle Hole, a good place to rest before the climb ahead.

❻ After the stile the coastal path continues directly on towards Beacon Hill; turn sharp right here and walk up the grassy track until you reach a gate and stile and a country road ahead.

❼ Cross the stile and turn right onto the country lane. The remainder of the walk is a gentle stroll back to Battisborough Cross along this quiet road. As you enter the hamlet, there is an ivy-covered derelict schoolhouse off to your left and, just a little further along, the turning you took to Mothecombe at the walk's start.

The Round House at the far end of Meadowsfoot Beach.

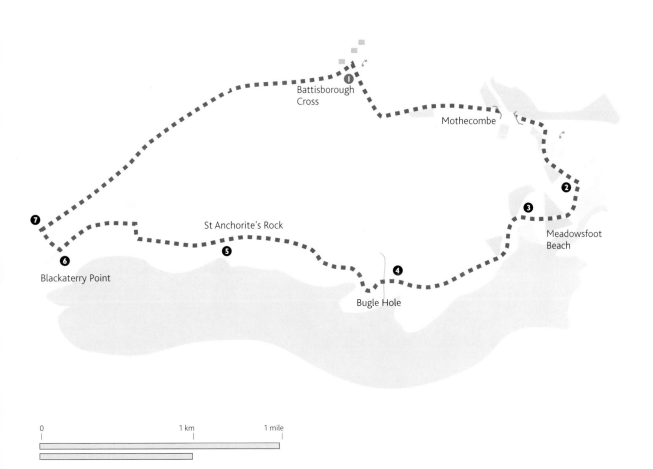

Battisborough Cross

Mothecombe

St Anchorite's Rock

Meadowsfoot Beach

Blackaterry Point

Bugle Hole

0   1 km   1 mile

▲ Map: Explorer 20

▲ Distance: 6 km/3¾ miles

▲ Walk ID: 339 Pete Brett

Difficulty rating

Time

▲ River, Toilets, National Trust/NTS, Wildlife

Saltram House Estate

The Saltram Estate has over 200 hectares of parkland including working farmland, woodlands and estuary shoreline with bird-watching hides. The gardens have magnificent specimen trees and were the setting for the film *Sense and Sensibility*.

❶ Join the footpath close to the vehicle exit from the supermarket, and walk under the subway and the A38. Turn right over the bridge and immediately right again to follow the tarmac path alongside the river, passing back under the A38 and over the railway line.

❷ At the footpath junction, go straight on and up through woodlands and gates into the grounds of Saltram House. Follow the metal fence on your right to the stable block and pass through the gate to visit the house, tearooms and National Trust shop.

❸ To continue the walk, go from the stable-block entrance through the car park and right into the overflow car park.

Turn right at the car park's entrance and descend along the estate road until you come to a gate leading to the estuary.

❹ Go through the gate onto the stony track. You pass a cottage on your left and come to a fork. Take the left fork and follow the wide track beside the estuary to the amphitheatre.

❺ From the amphitheatre you can look across the estuary to the white sails that mark the walk's start and end point. Continue along the track, past the bird-watching point on the left, to the gate.

❻ Pass through the gate and take the left fork in the path, ascending to rejoin the tarmac path. Retrace your steps to where you parked your car.

access information

Travelling from Exeter on the A38, take the Plymouth slip road and turn left at the traffic lights. Park close to Fort Crabtree.

For a shorter walk, park at Saltram House car park (fee payable).

further information

The Park at Saltram House Estate is open every day of the year. Phone 01752 333500 for information on opening times of the house, formal gardens, tearoom and shop.

Saltram House, a fine George II mansion with staterooms by Robert Adam. The gardens are separated from the park by a ha-ha, seen clearly in this aerial photograph.

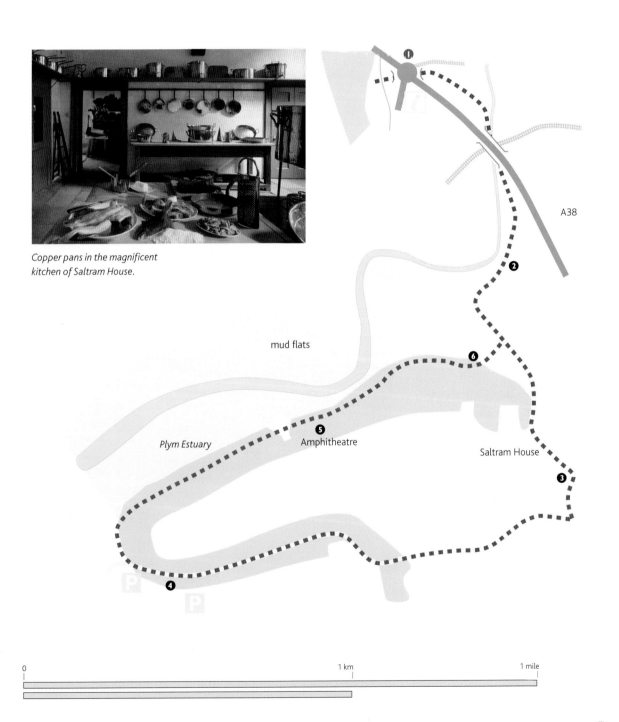

Copper pans in the magnificent kitchen of Saltram House.

A38

mud flats

Plym Estuary

Amphitheatre

Saltram House

0   1 km   1 mile

▲ Map: Explorer 105
▲ Distance: 7 km/4¼ miles
▲ Walk ID: 1513 Jim Grindle

Difficulty rating

Time

▲ River, Toilets, Stately Home,
National Trust, Wildlife, Birds, Good for
Kids, Nature Trail, Restaurant, Tea Shop,
Woodland, Ancient Monument

Lamouth Creek from Trelissick Garden

You begin by entering the park and dropping down to follow the river through woods to King Harry Ferry. The walk offers open views of the estuary before a gentle climb through the park back to the start.

1 Take the path next to the car park, signposted 'Woodland Walks'. Go through a gate next to a cattle grid and follow the path to a junction. Turn right onto the driveway and continue to the edge of a wood.

2 Go through the gate to the left of the cattle grid, then turn to the right on a path going uphill. Pass the lodge and go through the green gate. Cross the road and go through the gate on the other side. Follow a gravel track that zigzags downhill. When it straightens out there is a stream on the left.

3 Turn left and cross the stream. On the other side take the right fork, following Lamouth Creek, which is below you on your right. Continue as the woods thin out, until you reach the entrance to the next wood, marked by two low stone banks. Take the right fork, heading over the ditch and then straight through the rampart of the Iron Age fort before joining another track. Turn right. Just before the quay, go down a few steps and emerge into the open.

4 Visit Roundwood Quay, then retrace your steps back to point 3. Continue with the river now on your left for 1.5 km. You will reach a steep flight of steps leading down to the road you crossed earlier. The ferry is just to your left, and opposite is a white house with a flight of steps going up on its right.

5 At Bosanko's Cottage, take the track that continues on the far side. Only one track branches off to the right away from the river and your way is signposted. About 1.5 km from the ferry you leave the woods by a kissing gate. Go up the hill, keeping the iron fence on your right.

6 At the top cross the drive that enters Trelissick House. You will soon reach the exit from the car park. Go through the gate and back to the start.

access information

Trelissick is 6 km south of Truro on the B3289, east of the A39. Buses T7 and 89B run from Truro, where there is a railway station.

This footpath will lead you past cosy woodland cottages to the much grander residence of Trelissick House.

further information

The first house was built here in about 1750 and went through many hands, with much development of the gardens which were acquired by The National Trust in 1955.

Roundwood Quay was built in the 18th century to ship tin and copper, and in past days there were buildings for smelting and refining and many wharves. There was a malt house, limekilns and ship-building yards, a busy place compared to the tranquillity that you will find there now.

Since 1888 the King Harry Steam Ferry Company has operated a ferry that pulls itself across the Fal by chains, although the motive power is now diesel. It is thought that a ferry has existed here since the Norman Conquest.

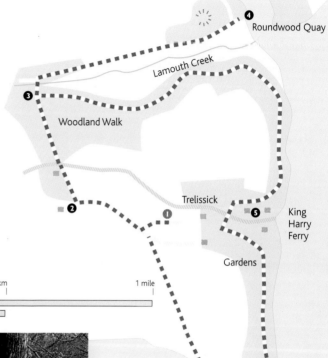

Roundwood Quay

Lamouth Creek

Woodland Walk

Trelissick

King Harry Ferry

Gardens

▲ Map: Explorer 106
▲ Distance: 11 km/6¾ miles
▲ Walk ID: 699 Pete Brett

Difficulty rating

Time

▲ Sea, Pub, Toilets, Museum, Church, Stately Home, Wildlife, Flowers, Great Views, Food Shop, Good for Kids, Tea Shop

South West Coast Path from Padstow

further information

The Elizabethan manor house of Prideaux Place has a deer park and is open to visitors in summer.

The church of St Petroc, dating mainly from the 15th century, and the Shipwreck Museum can both be found in Padstow.

This is a circular walk from the Cornish fishing port of Padstow, with long stretches of sandy beach ideal for swimming, and dramatic cliff-top views.

❶ Leave the car park on the path to the left of the toilet block and descend to the north side of the harbour. Join the South West Coast Path, which starts near the tourist information centre. The path ascends to the War Memorial with extensive views back towards Padstow and the Camel Estuary. Follow the path around Gun Point to the beautiful sandy Harbour Cove.

❷ Cross the sands to rejoin the path. At Hawker's Cove the path joins a short stretch of track behind the beach and skirts the old lifeboat house and terraced pilots' houses.

❸ Ascend from the pilots' houses over the stile and take the right path to Stone Daymark. Continue on the coast path above dramatic cliffs with outstanding views.

❹ At the stile, turn left inland to reach a road. Follow the road to the village of Crugmeer and curve round to the left at the junction. Pass the cottages on the left and take the next left turn.

❺ Take the footpath on the right, just past Little Crugmeer Farm. Cross the stile into the field. Cross diagonally over seven fields with slate stiles to a stile leading onto the road. Turn right along the road and under the arch to Prideaux Place. Continue down the road and turn left at the hotel into Fentonluna Lane. Descend through the town to the harbour. From the harbour return to the start via the road.

access information

Follow the A39 south from Wadebridge then take the A389 to Padstow. Do not descend into the town but continue for 200 m and turn into the top car park.

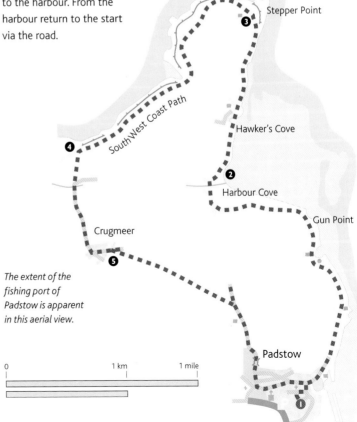

The extent of the fishing port of Padstow is apparent in this aerial view.

▲ Map: Explorer 111
▲ Distance: 3 km/1³/₄ miles
▲ Walk ID: 1095 Dennis Blackford

Difficulty rating

Time

▲ Hills or Fells, Sea, Toilets, Castle, National Trust, Wildlife, Birds, Flowers, Great Views, Butterflies, Restaurant, Tea Shop, Monument

Tintagel Castle and Coast

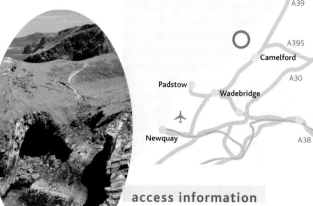

This walk goes through Tintagel and along the cliff path to visit the legendary castle of King Arthur and Merlin's Cave, with wonderful views and a wealth of wildlife.

❶ From the car park, turn right onto the main road and walk into Tintagel village. Walk through the village until reaching the 'No Through Road' at the side of the Cornishman's Inn. Follow this road down to the car park at the end.

❷ Follow the church wall around to the right and onto the coast path, looking out for the ruins of the castle below. Follow the path down.

❸ On reaching the paved path to the castle, take the path to your right which zigzags down to the Visitor Centre. At low tide you can go down to the beach and visit Merlin's Cave.

❹ Cross over the bridge and climb the steps to continue on the coast path up the other side of the valley. About 200 m further on, after crossing a little wooden bridge, follow the left-hand path up to Barras Nose, with its spectacular view over the cove and the castle. Continue on the coast path. About 1 km further on, pass through a gate which will lead you to Willapark. Pass through the gap in the wall and take the left-hand fork to the point. Return to the junction and

With natural and man-made rock formations, it is no wonder Tintagel is a place of legends.

continue on the path to the right of the gap, heading down into the valley.

❺ Take the steps up the other side of the valley and cross the stile down to the track. Turn right to return to the starting point.

access information

Tintagel is on the B3263 off the A39. From Tintagel, take the Boscastle road for about 1 km to Bossiney car park on your left.

There are also bus services to take you to Tintagel.

further information

At waymark 5, instead of turning right, you could turn left to detour down into the secluded cove of Bossiney Haven, which is popular for swimming at low tide.

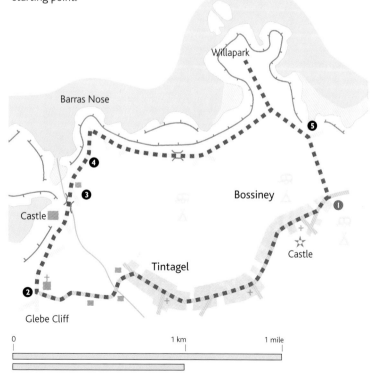

▲ Map: Explorer 106
▲ Distance: 6 km/3¾ miles
▲ Walk ID: 1869 Dennis Blackford

Difficulty rating

Time

▲ Hills or Fells, River, Pub, Toilets, Wildlife, Birds, Flowers, Great Views, Butterflies, Café, Gift Shop, Food Shop, Public Transport, Restaurant, Tea Shop, Woodland

Wadebridge Woods and River Camel

This route climbs high above Wadebridge through farmland to the quiet country lanes of the village of Burlawn, before dropping down again into the woods and joining the Camel Trail.

❶ From Wadebridge town follow the signs to the Camel Trail, where the walk begins. Ignore the Camel Trail itself and take the road that runs parallel to it on the right. Walk straight on, following the farm track up the hill that is signposted as a public footpath to Treraven. At the top of the track, go through the wooden gate and follow the right-hand field boundary, which leads you through another wooden gate and onto the farm track beyond.

❷ Walk up the farm track, ignoring the junction first left, until you reach Treraven farmhouse. At the farmhouse, turn left. Proceed for a few metres to the Y-junction, then bear right. The track takes you to the top of the hill, where it turns sharp left (the farmer sometimes puts string across this track to guide cattle), and after 200 m bears right again. Stay on the track until it joins a public road, then walk straight on for 200 m to a crossroads.

access information

The walk begins adjacent to the start of the Camel Trail. Drive to Wadebridge and park in Guineaport Road.

Travel by bus to Wadebridge, then walk along Guineaport Road to the start of the Camel Trail.

further information

There are toilets, food, pubs, restaurants, etc. in Wadebridge.

Most of the route follows easy ground and there are no stiles.

If you are walking with children or dogs, be aware that this trail is popular with cyclists.

The Camel Trail crosses and re-crosses the gently-flowing River Camel.

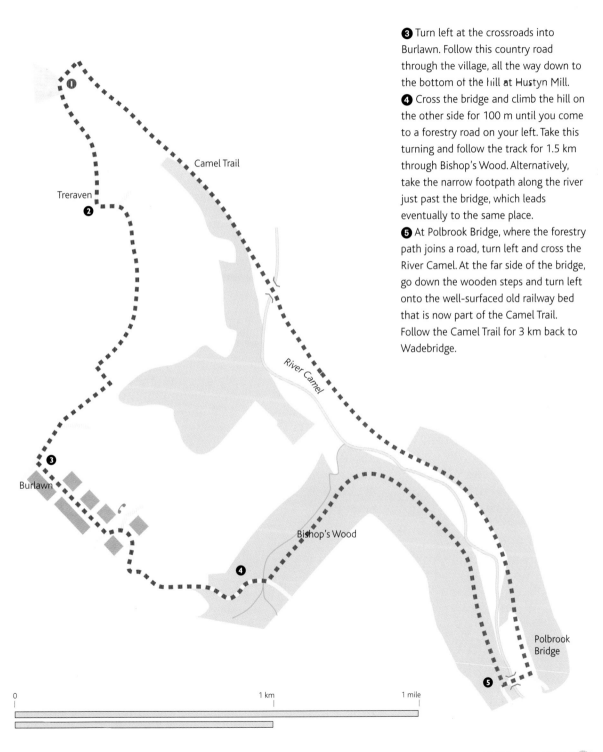

❸ Turn left at the crossroads into Burlawn. Follow this country road through the village, all the way down to the bottom of the hill at Hustyn Mill.

❹ Cross the bridge and climb the hill on the other side for 100 m until you come to a forestry road on your left. Take this turning and follow the track for 1.5 km through Bishop's Wood. Alternatively, take the narrow footpath along the river just past the bridge, which leads eventually to the same place.

❺ At Polbrook Bridge, where the forestry path joins a road, turn left and cross the River Camel. At the far side of the bridge, go down the wooden steps and turn left onto the well-surfaced old railway bed that is now part of the Camel Trail. Follow the Camel Trail for 3 km back to Wadebridge.

Camel Trail

Treraven ❷

River Camel

Burlawn ❸

Bishop's Wood

❹

Polbrook Bridge

❺

❶

| 0 | 1 km | 1 mile |

▲ Map: Explorer 111

▲ Distance: 9 km/5½ miles

▲ Walk ID: 1580 Dennis Blackford

Difficulty rating

👞👞👞

Time

● ● ● ●

▲ Hills or Fells, River, Sea, Pub, Toilets, Museum, Church, Castle, Birds, Flowers, Butterflies, Cafe, Gift Shop, Food Shop, Public Transport, Restaurant, Tea Shop

Bude Canal and Coast

This excellent walk begins at the seaside town of Bude, with its museum, castle and tranquil canal. Widemouth Beach makes for a pleasant stop-off, before the route continues along the spectacular coast, overlooking the town's sandy shoreline.

❶ Leave the car park and take the tarmac path along the canal's left bank. Ignore any turn-offs.

❷ When you come to Rodd's Bridge, cross to the right-hand bank and continue along the canal path. The path takes you past the remains of a higher lock and through a cycle restriction gate.

❸ Just past Helebridge, at the end of the tarmac path, pass through the gate by the signpost and continue along the grass track. Go over the stile at the end of the track and turn right onto the concrete road. You come to a second stile about 100 m up the road, to the left of the tearoom entrance. Cross this into the field, then follow the tractor path round to the right and on up the field to a stile in the hedge. Cross this third stile and proceed up the left-hand side of this field and the one that follows.

❹ Walk through the wide gap in the hedge, crossing a junction of tracks, which takes you diagonally into the next field. Follow the field's right-hand boundary towards the sea. Leave the boundary path when you reach the tractor track, and proceed until you reach the gate and the coast road at Salthouse.

❺ Cross the coast road and follow the path over to the sea. Head off to the left if you want some time on the beach or to use the facilities at Widemouth. The route continues to the right, along the rugged coast and through Phillip's Point nature reserve. At Upton the path takes you through a wooden gate and across a large field. Continue to follow the coast to the end of the fields. You then face a steep climb to the viewpoint at Efford Beacon. Follow the 'Acorn' posts with their yellow arrows.

❻ At the bottom of Efford Down, go through a wooden gate onto the grassland of Compass Point. You pass Compass Tower on your left. Follow the faint diagonal path across the grass to the right.

❼ Turn right onto the path that leads off the grass, towards Bude. Follow the path to its end and down left through a wooden gate to the road. The road leads you back along the canal to your start point. Alternatively, cross by the lock gates to the beach, or walk along the left bank of the canal to the museum and tearooms.

access information

The walk starts at Bude's main car park and tourist information office. However, parking here is expensive so we recommend leaving your car outside the Falcon Hotel across the bridge, or turning right towards the breakwater where there is usually plenty of parking space alongside the canal.

A39

A395

Camelford

Padstow

Wadebridge

A30

Bodmin

The spectacular rugged coastline at Bude.

further information

There are toilets at the car park and at the
halfway point at Widemouth Bay;
restaurants/tea shops at Bude, canal end and
Widemouth.

Wheelchair users have access along the
canal as far as Helebridge.

The free car park at the Bude end of
Widemouth Bay, near Phillip's Point, is an
alternative start point.

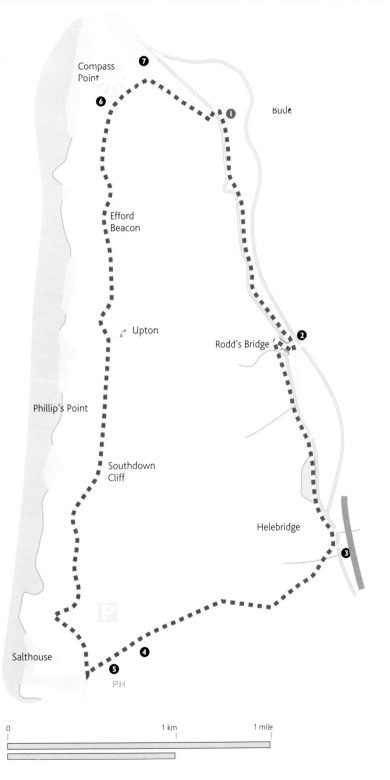

Compass Point

7

6

Bude

1

Efford
Beacon

Upton

Rodd's Bridge

2

Phillip's Point

Southdown
Cliff

Helebridge

3

Salthouse

4

5

PH

```
0                    1 km            1 mile
```

▲ Map: Explorer 111
▲ Distance: 4 km/2½ miles
▲ Walk ID: 1685 Dennis Blackford

Difficulty rating

Time

▲ River, Pub, Toilets, Church, Castle,
Wildlife, Birds, Butterflies, Café, Gift Shop,
Food Shop, Mostly Flat, Public Transport,
Nature Trail, Restaurant, Tea Shop

Bude Canal and Nature Reserve

This shorter, easier alternative to the coastal circuit on page 70 also begins with a stroll along Bude's canal, returning alongside the nature reserve where, in summer, you might be lucky enough to catch sight of great crested grebe.

1 Leave the car park and take the tarmac path along the canal's left bank. Ignore any turn-offs.

2 When you come to Rodd's Bridge, cross to the right-hand bank and continue along the canal path. The path takes you past the remains of a higher lock and through a cycle restriction gate.

3 At Helebridge, cross the canal and then the main road. Turn left and walk along the grass path at the side of the road for 100 m, where it joins a wide cycle path. Continue along this path.

4 When you come to the wide road to the water treatment plant, cross the main road and walk down the side road, which bears round to the right.

Dusk falls on the harbourside at Bude.

further information

There are toilets at the car park; food shops, restaurants/tea shops, museum, castle and gift shops at Bude.

Wheelchair users have access along the canal as far as Helebridge and also along the short path across the nature reserve (see waymark 6).

5 At the entrance to the water treatment works, take the path to the left of the main gate. Continue on this path, which leads you alongside the nature reserve.

6 Either take the path across the reserve, which leads to a viewing area and then joins the canal near our start point, or continue along the right-hand edge of the reserve. Where the track branches, follow the left branch to the start of the walk.

A disused lock on the Bude Canal.

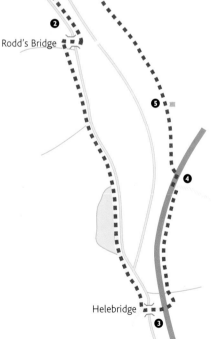

access information

The walk starts at Bude's main car park and tourist information office. Parking here is expensive, however, and we recommend leaving your car outside the Falcon Hotel across the bridge, or turning right towards the breakwater where there is usually plenty of parking space alongside the canal.

Rodd's Bridge

Helebridge

| 0 | | 1 km | 1 mile |

▲ Map: Explorer 111
▲ Distance: 4 km/2½ miles
▲ Walk ID: 1588 Dennis Blackford

Difficulty rating

Time

▲ Hills or Fells, Sea, Church, National Trust/NTS, Wildlife, Birds, Great Views, Butterflies, Moor, Woodland

Around St Genny's

Starting from the tiny village of St Genny's, this scenic route takes in some breathtaking stretches along the cliffs, and drops down into the valley with its contrasting meadows and heath land.

❶ Leave the car park and continue along the road towards the cottages. You soon come to a path on your left, signposted by The National Trust. Follow the path up the wooden steps on to the track. The track curves round to the right before reaching a wide gate with a kissing gate alongside. Pass through the kissing gate and follow the farm track around the right-hand edge of the field.

❷ At the end of the field, pass through a second kissing gate onto the cliff headland. Cross the field, bearing slightly right until you come to a fence and gate near the cliff edge.

❸ To admire the views over Crackington Haven Bay, go through the gate onto the headland. There are seats here if you want to take a break. Then return to the gate and walk by the fence along the cliff top. Follow the signs down through the field, bearing right, until you come to another kissing gate in the fence. Go through the gate and walk down the zigzag path and steps to the wooden bridge at the bottom.

❹ Cross over the bridge and the stile on the other side into the National Trust area of Cleave. Climb the steep zigzag path up the side of the valley. At the top of the slope, the path leads you along the cliff top.

❺ After the path begins to climb again, look out for a signpost with a small white arrow pointing to St Genny's via a small steep path on the right. Take this path down into the valley through the woodland.

❻ Cross the bridge over the stream at the bottom and continue up the hill on the other side. Walk through the meadow – there is no definite marked path – towards the gate at the far right-hand corner.

❼ Go through the gate or over the stile, then proceed up the metalled drive, crossing another metalled drive and onwards up a wide dirt track. Turn right where this track meets the drive further up, and follow the drive to the road. Turn right again to the car park, a few metres away.

access information

Take the A39 to Wainhouse Corner about 13 km south of Bude, and turn off towards Crackington Haven. A little way past the crossroads signposted Dizzard 1½ and Millock 3, there is a road to the right to St Genny's. Follow this road until you come to the parking area on the right-hand side of the road just before St Genny's church.

Crackington Haven Bay can be seen from the headland (see waymark 3).

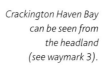

further information

There are no local facilities.

The views from the cliffs are spectacular, but the drop down is considerable. Children and dogs should be closely supervised.

Good walking boots or shoes with a good tread are advised, as there are some steep sections.

The coastline near to St Genny's.

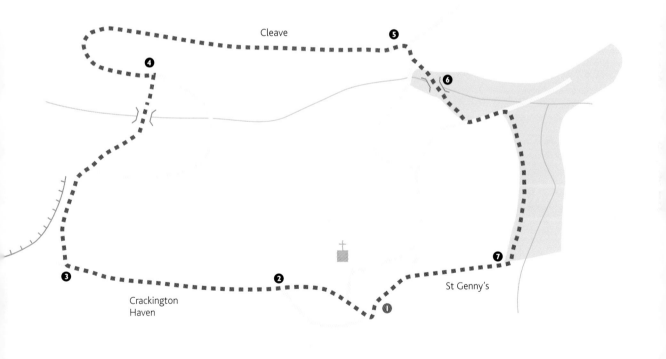

▲ Map: Explorer 9
▲ Distance: 7 km/4¼ miles
▲ Walk ID: 1346 Paul Edney

Difficulty rating

Time

▲ Lake/Loch, Toilets, Play Area, Birds, Great Views, Café

Haddon Hill from Wimbleball Lake

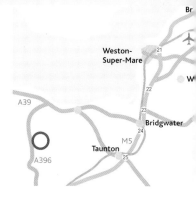

This walk passes Wimbleball Dam and continues up Haddon Hill, from where the views of Wimbleball Lake are superb. You descend through heath and woodland to return along the lakeside.

1 Leave the car park by the gate to the left of the tearoom and turn left onto the road. At the sign for the sailing club, 200 m along, continue on up the 'no through road'. When you reach the sharp left-hand bend, take the track on the right past the farm buildings, through a gate and down a paved track.

2 At the Y-junction, go through the left-hand gate and down the concrete road towards the dam. At the dam, turn right across the dam wall. Once across, turn right at the T-junction onto the road signposted to Bury.

3 After about 150 m, you come to some steep steps in the wall on your left, signposted 'Footpath to Haddon Hill'. Walk up the steps to the path and proceed through the trees. The path ends at a stile in a wire fence. Cross the stile and turn right onto the wide gravel path. After about 10 m, you come to heathland. Make your way up the faint path in a zigzag to the highest point.

4 Hadborough triangulation point at the top is set back in a patch of heather and gorse bushes. Turn left here and follow the wide path gently downhill across the heath. Continue past Haddon Hill car park, keeping ahead on the main path.

5 When you reach the tarmac road, cross over to the path. After about 20 m, you come to a faint crossroads. Turn left and follow the path downhill, first alongside gorse bushes, then through sparse woodland. When you meet the wider path, cross over and continue on the narrow path down through the trees.

6 Near the bottom of the hill, just above the lake, turn left onto the bridleway, following the sign to Dam and Bury. Continue until the bridleway joins the road, the same road you crossed at the top of the hill. Turn right towards Wimbleball Dam and Bury.

7 At the dam, turn right and right again at the far side, over the stile onto the grassy path above the lake. Follow the path through the trees, across the fields then over the bridge. Ignore the gate to the farm on the left and keep on the grassy path, heading off to the right.

further information

There are picnic tables, a tearoom, children's play area, toilets and telephone at the car park at the South West Lakes Trust site. Opening times are seasonal. There are also toilets at the Haddon Hill car park.

access information

The walk starts at the pay-and-display car park at the South West Lakes Trust site.

Wimbleball Lake. The dam, seen from the bridleway, above; and a closer view of the lake through the trees at waymark 7.

8 Keep following the path until you reach the sailing club on your left. At the gate above the club, turn left onto the track ahead. Walk past the children's play area, up through the gate onto the main road. Turn right at the road and walk the 200 m back to the start.

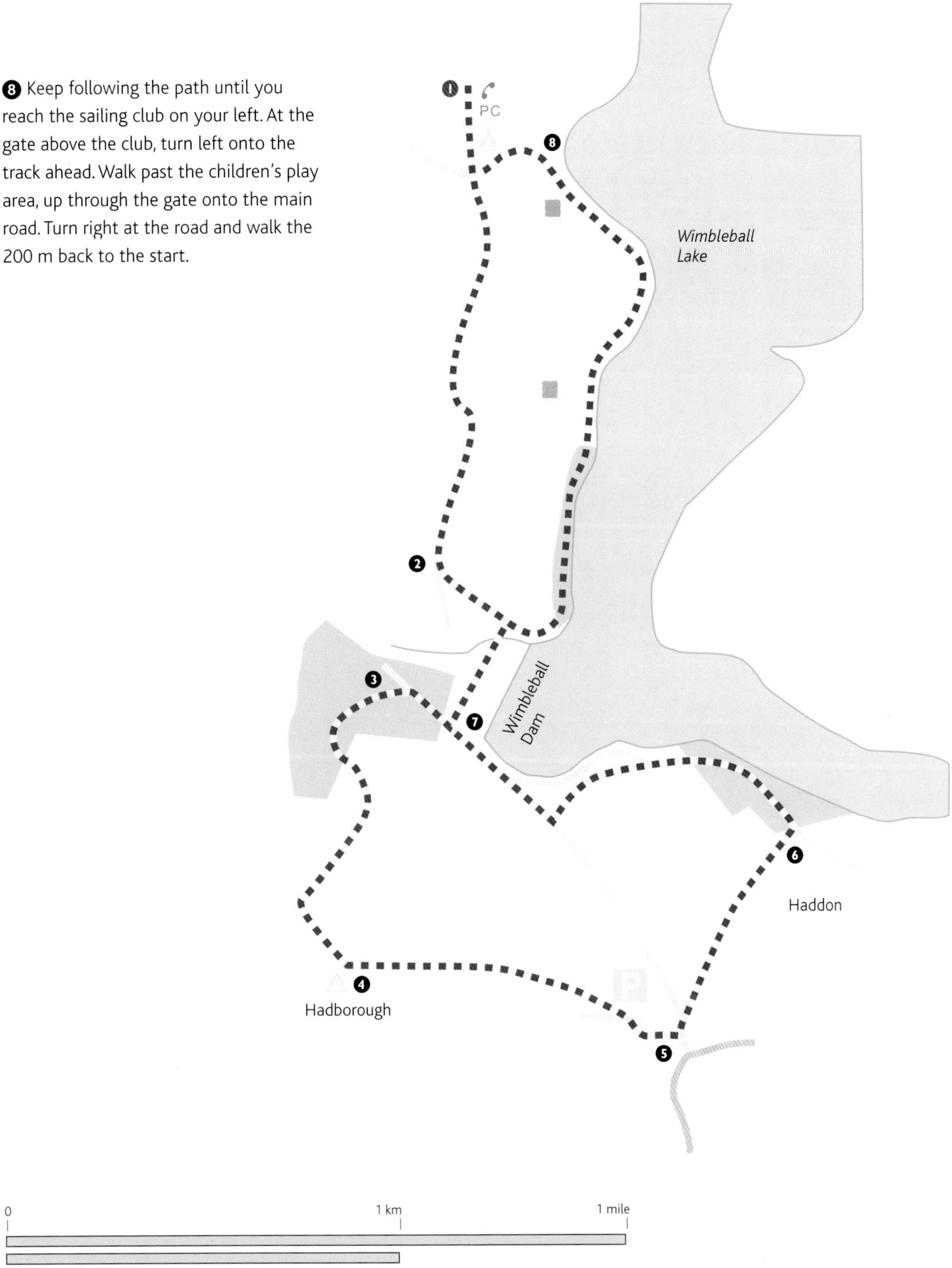

Wimbleball Lake

PC

1

8

2

3

7

Wimbleball Dam

6

Haddon

4

Hadborough

5

0   1 km   1 mile

▲ Map: Explorer 155
▲ Distance: 10 km/6¼ miles
▲ Walk ID: 2068 Pat Roberts

Difficulty rating

Time

▲ Hills or Fells, River, Wildlife, Birds, Flowers, Great Views, Butterflies, Woodland

Dundas Aqueduct and Warleigh Wood from Brown's Folly

This interesting walk begins at Brown's Folly nature reserve, and includes a stretch along the Kennet and Avon Canal to Dundas Aqueduct.

❶ Walk to the back of the car park and head west through the trees. You emerge on a wide track junction. Turn right, following the sign to the Pepperpot Trail, then pass through an iron kissing gate onto open grassland.

❷ At the end of the grassland, the trail veers left up to a fence. Go through the gate in the fence and continue on through the trees. Gradually make your way down to the A363, then turn left along the verge.

❸ At the 'Wiltshire' sign, cross the road and climb over the wall to follow the signposted footpath. After about 80 m, turn sharp right and down. Where you meet another track, turn left. Continue down, past a wooden seat on the right, then round a metal gate to reach a narrow road. Turn right down the road and walk around the bend.

❹ Turn left onto the signposted track, proceed past the first house, then cross over a yard to take the path down between the two fences to the waterside fields. Walk along the waterway until you near the aqueduct, when the path veers away from the water to a stile at the left of a building.

Few sights could be more picturesque than the view of a narrowboat drifting serenely along the Kennet and Avon Canal.

5 Cross the stile and climb the flight of steps. To explore the aqueduct and Visitor Centre on the other side of the canal, turn right. To resume the walk, return to this point and turn left. Climb up the sunken path through the trees. The path eventually levels out and swings right. Look out for a narrow path off to the left. Proceed along this path up to a narrow road, then turn left again.

6 At the junction with the road, turn left and follow the sign to Bathford. Turn left at the narrow road signposted to Watleigh and stay with the road until it swings slightly left and starts to drop. At this point, cross the stile on the right into the woodland. Follow the path, ignoring any junctions, until you come to another stile. Cross over into the field and walk ahead with the hedge on your right. Where you rejoin the A363, turn left.

7 Pass the signs for Bath and Somerset, then turn right back up the footpath onto Bathford Hill, pass the information board and, at the first fork, take the path to the left marked Pepperpot Trail. At the next fork, leave the trail and go right. Continue on, through the gate onto the open grassland, and then back through the woodland to the start point.

further information

The limestone underlying Brown's Folly dates back millions of years. Mined since Roman times, the area is riddled with caves and underground workings. Above ground, wild flowers and butterflies flourish.

access information

The walk begins at the car park of Brown's Folly. From the A4 turn south onto the A363 and immediately left to Bathford. After the third 'priority road control', turn right up a narrow steep road. The road swings left and the car park is on the right.

0   1 km   1 mile

Index

acknowledgements

The publishers wish to thank the following for the kind use of their pictures:
Front cover: TL Bob Krist/Corbis. Back cover, TL John Thorn, BL Paul Edney.
Dennis Blackford: pp. 26, 33, 54 all, 57, 59, 73, 74, 75; **Collections:** pp. 56 Angela Hampton, 58 Roy Westlake; **Corbis:** pp. 10 Adam Woolfitt, 11 Clay Perry, 12 Bob Krist, 16 David Dixon/Papilio, 18 Yann Artus-Bertrand, 20/21 Angelo Hornak, 22 Robert Estall, 24 Michael Busselle, 30 Bob Krist, 32 Patrick Ward, 38 Roger Tidman, 42 Nick Hawkes/Ecoscene, 46 Yann Artus-Bertrand, 48 Adam Woolfitt, 49 Bob Krist, 50 Michael Busselle, 51 John Farmer/Ecoscene, 52, 63 + 64/65 Michael Boys, 66 Jason Hawkes, 67 Bob Krist, 78 Kristi J Black; **Paul Edney:** pp. 31, 76 both; **Getty-Images:** pp. 14 Fergus O'Brien/Taxi, 44 Michael Busselle/Stone, Chris Simpson/Stone; **Hutchison Picture Library:** pp. 13 P.W. Rippon, 34 Liba Taylor; **The Lanaways:** pp. 29, 36, 37, 68; **Molyneaux Associates:** p. 72; **Dave Pawley:** pp. 60, 61; **Wendy Pickler:** p.8; **John Thorn:** p. 40.